Lost & found

TEN EVANGELISTIC SERMONS
by Charles H. Spurgeon

Also Updated by the Editor

Charles Haddon Spurgeon

366 Daily Readings from Most Things Spurgeon (December 2018)

According to Promise: *The Lord's Method of Dealing with His Chosen People*

All of Grace (including larger print paperback)

Peace and Purpose in Trial and Suffering

Spurgeon's Catechism (January 2019)

The Clue of the Maze: 70 Daily Readings for Conquering Doubt

The Imprecatory *Psalms from Spurgeon's The Treasury of David* (February 2019)

The New Spurgeon's Devotional Bible: A 600,000 Word Two Year Devotional

The Penitential Psalms *from Spurgeon's The Treasury of David* (July 2021)

The Soul Winner (August 2019)

Spurgeon's Sermons Series

3:16: Thirteen Selected Sermons

A Defense of Calvinism (January 2019)

A Sower Went Out to Sow: *Nine Sermons on The Parable of the Sower*

Other Works

Sermons of D. L. Moody: 21 Sermons

The Fear of God, by John Bunyan

The Reformed Pastor, by Richard Baxter (April 2019)

Contact Information

MostThingsSpurgeon@gmail.com

www.goo.gl/kLbXcU

ACKNOWLEDGMENTS

My sister, Laura, can be competent, brutal, friendly and encouraging at the same time. Pity the reader who must suffer through books written by authors who do not have someone like her proofreading their manuscripts.

My wife, Patti, read each sermon, making comments and suggestions and giving encouragement. She also suggested Spurgeon's message on Job 13:10 after quoting from it while speaking at a ladies retreat.

A completed manuscript is just the beginning! Our daughter, Amber, designed the cover, did the formatting for the eBook, and the layout for the print edition. These are no simple tasks! I give her Five-Stars

Contents

INTRODUCTION

These ten sermons were selected for their gospel content. For those unsaved, our hope and prayer is that God will use these to your salvation in Christ Jesus. For Christians, may you find comfort and encouragement. For preachers, may you find outline suggestions, illustrations you can adapt, and a click on the refresh button for your gospel preaching efforts.

A SIMPLE SERMON
FOR SEEKING SOULS

A Sermon Delivered
by C. H. Spurgeon on Sunday Morning, July 12, 1857
to an audience of over 10,000
at the Music Hall, Royal Surrey Gardens, London

Romans 10:8-13

"The word is near you, in your mouth and in your heart" (that is, the word of faith that we proclaim); because, if you confess with your mouth that Jesus is Lord and believe in your heart that God raised him from the dead, you will be saved. For the Scripture says, "Everyone who believes in him will not be put to shame." For there is no distinction between Jew and Greek; the same Lord is Lord of all, bestowing his riches on all who call on him. For **"everyone who calls on the name of the Lord will be saved."**

Introduction

A respected theologian has said that many of us preach the word of God and assume our hearers have more knowledge on our subject than they actually do. He says, "there are very often people in the congregation who are completely unfamiliar with theology." They are total strangers to the whole process of grace and salvation. It is appropriate, then, for the preacher to sometimes speak to his hearers as if they were totally unaware of what he is talking about. "Because," says this good man, "it is better to suppose too little knowledge, and so explain the thing clearly, to the lowest understanding, than to suppose too much, and so let the uninformed escape without a word of instruction."

Now, I think I will not make that mistake this morning, because I will assume that at least some in my congregation are completely uninformed about the great plan of salvation. I am sure that you who know the gospel well, and have experienced its preciousness, will bear with me while I try to tell the story, in the simplest way possible, of how people are lost, and how they are saved by calling on the name of the Lord.

Well then, we must begin at the beginning. Our text speaks of people being saved, so it implies that people need saving. If they had been as God created them, they would not need saving. Adam in the Garden of Eden did not need saving. He was perfect, pure, clean, holy, and acceptable before God. He was our representative. He stood as the representative for the entire human race when he touched the forbidden fruit and ate of the tree of which God said, "You shall not eat, for in the day that you eat of it you shall surely die."

When he disobeyed God in that way, he needed a Savior. And we, as his offspring through his sin, are born into this world also each needing a Savior. But we who are here this morning cannot throw all the blame on Adam. No one has ever been damned or ever will be only because of Adam's sin. Children dying in infancy are, without doubt, saved by sovereign grace through the atonement that is in Christ Jesus. No sooner do they close their eyes to earth, being innocent of any actual sin, than they immediately open them to the joy of heaven.

But you and I are not children. We do not need to talk about Adam's sins right now. We have our own to deal with and God knows they are enough to condemn us. The Bible tells us that we have all "sinned and fall short of the glory of God," and our conscience bears witness to the same truth. We have all broken the great commands of God and the result is that the righteous God is bound to punish us for the sins we have committed.

Now, my brothers and sisters, it is because you and I have broken God's law and are subject to his divine wrath, that we stand here in need of mercy. Therefore every one of us, if we want to be truly happy, if we want to live in heaven with God forever, must be saved.

But there is a lot of confusion in the minds of many of what being saved means. Allow me, then, just to say, that salvation means two things. In the first place, it means escaping from the punishment of the sins we have committed. In the next place, it means escaping from the habit of sinning, so that in the future we will not live as we once did. The way that God saves you is twofold. First, he says, "I forgive you, I will not punish you. I have punished Christ instead of you. You will be saved."

But that is only half the work. Next, he says, "I will not let you go on sinning as you have been in the habit of doing. I will give you a new heart that will hold back your evil habits. Until now you have been a slave of sin. You will now be free to serve me. Come away. You are not going to serve that dark master of yours any more. You must leave that demon. From now on you will be my child and my servant. Do not say, 'I cannot do that.' Come to me. I will give you grace to do it. I will give you grace to break away from drunkenness, grace to stop swearing, grace to quit disrespecting my holy day. I will give you grace to keep my commandments and be delighted in doing so."

I repeat, salvation is made up of two things. One is being freed from the habit of living in opposition to God. The other is being delivered from the punishment that opposition brings on.

Our great subject this morning is, how people are saved. I shall attempt to speak on our subject using very plain language, with no attempt to dress it with eloquent words. What is it to be saved? That is the one great question. A Christian understands being saved as having new thoughts, a new mind, a new heart, and then, to have a new home forever at God's right hand in perfect happiness. How is a person saved? "What must I do to be saved?" is a cry springing from many lips here this morning. The answer in our text is this, "Everyone who calls on the name of the Lord will be saved."

I will first try to explain the text a little—*explanation*. Second, I will try to free the text from some errors about salvation, that are very popular—that will be *refutation*. And then third, I will plead the usefulness of my text upon your minds. That will be—*pleading. Explanation, refutation, pleading*. You will remember these points. May God impress them upon your mind!

Explanation

First, then, EXPLANATION. What is meant by calling on the name of the Lord? I tremble at this very moment, because I believe it is very easy to be confusing when words are used carelessly. Many times a preacher's explanations hide the meaning of Scripture instead of making it clearer. Many times it seems the preacher is like a painted window that shuts out the light, instead of letting it in. How are we to answer that simple question? I have given that a lot of thought. What is faith? What is believing? What is calling on the name of the Lord?

In order to get the true sense of this, I turned to my concordance and looked up the passages where the same word is used. As far as I can gather, I may say from the authority of Scripture, that the word "call" means *worship*. So we might translate the passage, "Everyone who worships God will be saved." But you must let me explain how the word "worship" is used in the Bible in order to explain the word "call."

In the first place, to call on the name of the Lord means to *worship God*. You will find in the book of Genesis that "when man began to multiply on the face of the land," that "people began to call upon the name of the LORD." That is, they began to worship God. They built altars in his name. They demonstrated their belief in the sacrifice that was to come by offering a representative sacrifice on the altars they built. They bowed their knees in prayer and lifted their voices in holy song and cried, "Great is Jehovah, Creator, Preserver, let him be praised, world without end."

Now, whoever in this wide, wide world who is given the grace to worship God, in God's way, will be saved. If you worship him through Jesus, and have faith in the atonement of the cross, if you worship God by humble prayer and wholehearted praise, your worship is a proof that you will be saved. You could not worship like that unless you had grace in your heart. Your faith and grace are a proof that you will be in heaven. Whoever on this earth who worships God in humble devotion will be saved. Wherever they are, whether in God's house or out of it, whoever will sincerely worship God with a pure heart, looking for acceptance through the atonement of Christ, and humbly throws himself on the mercy of God, will be saved. That is the promise.

But just so no one should run away with a mistaken idea of what worship is, we must explain just a little more. The word "call" in holy Scripture means *prayer*. You remember the story of Elijah. When the prophets of Baal prayed to their false god for rain during the drought, Elijah said, "I will call upon the name of the LORD." When Elijah prayed for rain, "the heavens grew black with clouds and wind, and there was a great rain."

Whoever prays to God through Christ, with sincere prayer, will be saved. Oh, I can remember how this passage cheered me once. I felt the weight of sin and I did not know the Savior. I thought God would blast me with his wrath and strike me with his hot displeasure! I went from chapel to chapel to hear the word preached, but I never heard the gospel. I believe I would have been driven to suicide through grief and sorrow, but then I heard these sweet words, "Everyone who calls on the name of the Lord will be saved."

Well, I thought, I cannot believe on Christ as I could wish. I cannot find pardon, but I know I call on his name. I know I pray. Yes, I pray with groans and tears and sighs day and night. If I am ever lost, I will plead that promise: "Oh God, you said, the one who calls on your name will be saved. I did call. Will you cast me away? I did plead your promise. I did lift up my heart in prayer. Can you be righteous and yet damn the person who really did pray?"

Prayer is the forerunner of salvation. Keep that sweet thought. Sinner, you cannot pray and perish. Praying and perishing are two things that never go together. Prayer can come in many ways. It may be a groan. It may be a tear or a prayer without words. It may be ungrammatical and harsh to the ear. But if it is a prayer from the innermost heart, you will be saved. Otherwise this promise is a lie. As surely as you pray, whoever you may be, whatever your past life, whatever the sins that you indulged, even if they are the worst that pollute mankind, yet if you have learned to pray from your heart, you cannot perish, because God lives in you. "Everyone who calls on the name of the Lord will be saved."

But the word "call" means a little more. It indicates *trust*. No one can call on the name of the Lord unless they trust in that name. We must have faith in the name of Christ or else we have not called properly. Listen, then, poor tried sinner. You have come here this morning aware of your guilt, awakened to your danger. Here is your answer. Christ Jesus the Son of God became a man. He was "born of the virgin Mary, suffered under Pontius Pilate, was crucified, dead and buried." He did this to save sinners like you. Will you believe this? Will you trust your soul to it? Will you say, "Sink or swim, Christ Jesus is my hope and if I perish I will perish with my arms around his cross, crying:

> 'Nothing in my hands I bring
> Simply to the cross I cling'"?

Poor miserable soul, if you can do that, you will be saved. Come, now. No good works of yours are needed, no sacraments. He only asks from you what he has already given you. You are nothing, will you take Christ to be everything? Come, you are dirty with sin, will you be washed? Will you get down on your knees and cry, "Lord, have mercy on me, a sinner. Not for anything I have done or can do, but for the sake of Jesus, whose blood streamed from his hands and feet, and in whom alone I trust"?

Why sinner, the universe will collapse, heaven will be emptied, and God would be no more rather than the promise would be broken to anyone in the world who calls on the name of the Lord. The person who trusts in Christ and calls on his name will be saved!

One more thing and then I think I will have given you the entire Scripture meaning of this word. Calling on the name of the Lord means *professing his name*. Do you remember what Ananias said to Saul, afterwards called Paul? "Rise and be baptized and wash away your sins, calling on his name." Now, sinner, if you would be obedient to Christ's word, Christ's word says, "Whoever believes and is *immersed* will be saved. Notice that I translated that word "baptize." Most Bibles do not actually translate it. I would be unfaithful to my knowledge of God's word if I did not translate it for you.

If it means sprinkle, then let it be translated "sprinkle." But our translators would not dare to do that. They know they have nothing in all classical language that would ever justify them doing that and they are not brash enough to attempt it. But I dare to translate it, "Whoever believes and is immersed will be saved." And though immersion is nothing, yet God requires those who believe to be immersed, in order to make a profession of their belief.

I repeat, immersion is nothing in salvation, but it is the profession of salvation that God requires of every person who puts their trust in the Savior. When Jesus came to John to be baptized by him, John would have prevented him, but Jesus said to him, "it is fitting for us to fulfill all righteousness." And our Savior commands those who put their trust in him to also "fulfill all righteousness." Jesus went meekly down from the shore of the Jordan River to be immersed beneath the waves; therefore let every believer be baptized in his name.

Now some of you draw back from the thought of making a profession. "No," you say, "we will believe and be secret Christians." Then hear the words of the Lord Jesus Christ: "Whoever is ashamed of me and of my words, of him will the Son of Man be ashamed when he comes in his glory and the glory of the Father, and of the holy angels." I will state the obvious; not one of you in your entire life ever knew a secret Christian and I will prove it. If you knew someone was a Christian, then it could not be a secret. If it was a secret, then how did you find out? So, since you never knew a secret Christian, you are not justified in believing there ever was such a person.

What would a Commander-in-Chief think of his soldiers, if they should swear they were loyal and true, and were to say, "Sir, we prefer to not wear these uniforms, let us dress as civilians! We are very honest and upright men, but we do not want to stand in your ranks and be recognized as your soldiers. We would rather slink into the enemy's camp, and into your camps too, and not wear anything that would show that we were your soldiers!" Ah! Some of you do the same thing with Christ. You are going to be secret Christians, are you, and sneak into the devil's camp, and into Christ's camp, but not be recognized by anyone?

Well, if you are determined to take that chance, you will do so, but I would not like to risk it. It is a solemn threatening; "of him will the Son of Man be ashamed when he comes in his glory and the glory of the Father, and of the holy angels!" It is a very serious thing when Christ says, "If anyone would come after me, let him deny himself and take up his cross daily and follow me." I say to every sinner here whom God has awakened to feel his need of a Savior, obedience to the commands of Christ is not an option; not on this point or any other.

Hear the way of salvation: Worship, Prayer, Faith, Profession. And if people would be obedient in professing Christ, they would follow the Bible and be baptized in water, in the name of the Father, of the Son, and of the Holy Spirit. God requires this. People are saved without any baptism, and multitudes go to heaven who are never washed in the water, and though baptism does not save, yet if anyone would be saved, they must not be disobedient. And because God gives a command, I am required to enforce it. Jesus said, "Go into all the world and proclaim the gospel to the whole creation. Whoever believes and is baptized will be saved, but whoever does not believe will be condemned."

This is my explanation of my text. No member of the Church of England can object to my interpretation. Their own documents support dipping. They only say that if children are unhealthy they are to be sprinkled. And it is marvelous how many sickly children have been born lately. I am astonished to find any of you alive where so much weakness has existed! The dear little ones are so tender, that a few drops is enough instead of the dipping that their own church recommends. I recommend that all members of that church would be better, if they would be more consistent with their own articles of faith. They would also be more consistent with Scripture. If your children are unhealthy, then you can allow them to be sprinkled. But if you are good members of your church you will have them immersed if they can be without danger.

Refutation

Our second point is REFUTATION. There are some popular errors about salvation that need to be dealt with by being proved wrong. My text says, "everyone who calls on the name of the Lord will be saved."

Now, one idea that conflicts with my text is that it is absolutely necessary that a priest or a minister needs to be present to assist people in their salvation. This idea is alive and well in other places besides just the Roman Catholic Church. There are many, sadly, too many, who make evangelical ministers as much their priest as the Catholic makes their priest their helper. There are many who imagine that salvation cannot be accomplished except in some undefinable and mysterious way. They insist that the pastor or priest must be involved with it.

Hear this then, if you had never seen a pastor in your lives, if you had never heard the voice of the bishop or elder of the church, yet if you did call on the name of the Lord your salvation would be just as certain without one as with one. People cannot call on a God they do not know. The preacher exists to explain the way to be saved. How can the unsaved call on the Lord unless they know who he is? "How are they to believe in him of whom they have never heard? And how are they to hear without someone preaching?" But that is where the office of preacher ends. Our job is to tell the message. After that, God the Holy Spirit must apply it.

Beware of priestcraft. And beware of man-craft, and minister-craft, and pastor-craft, and clergy-craft. All God's people are clergy. That is, all who are saved have been anointed with the Holy Spirit. A distinction between clergy and laity should never have been made. All who love the Lord Jesus Christ are clergy and are as much qualified to preach the gospel as any person alive. If God has given you the ability and called you to the work by his Spirit, then no ordination by men is necessary. If the call of God's Spirit in the heart directs us to proclaim his truth, we do not need the laying on of the hands of a priest or a body of elders to do so.

Brothers and sisters, understand that neither Paul, nor an angel from heaven, nor Apollos, nor Peter can help you in salvation. No man, nor men, nor Pope, nor Archbishop, nor bishop, nor priest, nor pastor, nor anyone else has grace enough to give to others. Each one of us must go on our own to the one source, pleading this promise, "Everyone who calls on the name of the Lord will be saved." If I was stuck in a coal mine in Siberia, where I could never hear the gospel, and if I did call on the name of Christ, the road to heaven is just as straight without the minister as with him. The path to heaven is just as clear from the wilds of Africa and from the prison as it is from this meeting house where the gospel is preached. Still, for education and encouragement, all Christians love the ministry. They do not trust in the priest or the preacher for salvation, but the word of God is sweet to them. "How beautiful are the feet of those who preach the good news!"

Another very common error is, that a good dream is a most splendid thing in order to save people. Some of you do not know how widespread this error is. I do. Many people believe that if you dream that you see the Lord in the night you will be saved. Or, that if you can see him on the cross, or if you think you see some angels, or if you dream that God says to you, "You are forgiven," then all is well. But if you do not have a very nice dream you cannot be saved.

Some people really believe this. Now, if this is true, then the sooner we all become addicted to painkillers the better, because there is nothing that makes people drowsy and hallucinate like these drugs. If this were true, then every pastor should open a pharmacy and distribute lots of painkillers and then his people would all dream themselves into heaven. But let us dismiss this nonsense, there is nothing to it. Dreams are the confused mess of a wild imagination, the shaky foundation of ridiculous ideas. How can they be the way to be saved?

Rowland Hill, the famous open air preacher, has a good answer. I must quote it for lack of a better one. When a woman claimed that she was saved because she dreamed, he said, "Well, my good woman, it is very nice to have good dreams when you are asleep, but I want to see how you act when you are awake. If your conduct is not consistent with holy living when you are awake, I will not give a snap of the fingers for your dreams." Ah, I am amazed that any person could be so foolish as to tell me the stories that I have heard myself about dreams. Poor dear creatures. When they were sound asleep they saw the gates of heaven open, and a white angel came and washed their sins away, and then they saw that they were pardoned, and since then they have never had a doubt or a fear. Well, it is time that you should begin to doubt, a very good time that you should doubt, because if that is all the hope you have, it is a poor one. Remember, it is, "everyone who calls on the name of the Lord will be saved."

Dreams may have some value. Sometimes people have been frightened out of their senses by them and they became the better for them. Charles Dickens' Ebenezer Scrooge in *A Christmas Carol* is not without support in real life. Again, some people have become alarmed by dreams into spiritual awakening. But to trust in a dream is to trust a shadow, to build your hopes on bubbles that need barely a puff of wind to burst them into nothingness. Oh! Remember you do not need a vision or a remarkable dream. If you have had one, you do not need to ignore it. It may have helped you. But do not trust in it. And if you have never had one, remember it is not necessary. Simply calling on God's name comes with the promise of salvation attached to it.

Now there are others of you, you are a good sort of people too, and you have been laughing while I have been talking about dreams. It is now time to take our turn to laugh at you. There are some people who think they must have some very wonderful kind of feelings, or else they cannot be saved. Or they must have some most extraordinary thoughts such as they have never had before or else they certainly cannot be saved.

A woman once applied to me for church membership, So I asked her whether she had ever had a change of heart. She said, "Oh yes sir. Such a change as you must be familiar with," she said, "I felt it across my chest in a special way, sir. When I was praying one day I felt as if I did not know what was the matter with me, I felt so different. And when I went to the chapel, sir, one night, I came away and felt so different from what I felt before, so light." "Yes," I said, "light-headed, my dear soul, that is what you felt, but nothing more, I am afraid." The good woman was sincere enough. She thought it was all right with her, because something had affected her lungs, or in some way stirred her physically.

"No," I hear some of you say, "people cannot be so stupid as this." I assure you that if you could read the hearts of this congregation this morning, you would find there are hundreds here that have no better hope of heaven than that. I am dealing with a very popular objection right now. "I thought," someone said to me one day, "I thought when I was in the garden, that Christ could take my sins away just as easily as he could move the clouds. Do you know, sir, a moment or two later the cloud was all gone and the sun was shining. I thought to myself, the Lord is blotting out my sin." You may say to me that such a ridiculous thought as that cannot occur often. I tell you, it does. Indeed, it happens very frequently.

People get to thinking that the biggest nonsense in all the earth is a sign of divine grace in their hearts. Now, the only feeling I ever want to have is just this: I want to feel that I am a sinner and that Christ is my Savior. You may keep your visions, and dreams, and experiences, and excitements to yourselves. The only feeling that I desire to have is deep repentance and humble faith. And poor sinner, if you have that, you are saved.

Why, some of you believe you must have some kind of electric shock or some very wonderful thing go all through you from head to foot before you can be saved. Now hear this, "The word is near you, in your mouth and in your heart." "If you confess with your mouth that Jesus is Lord and believe in your heart that God raised him from the dead, you will be saved." Why do you want all this nonsense about dreams and supernatural thoughts? All that is needed is that, as a guilty sinner, I come and throw myself on Christ. When that is done, the soul is safe. All the visions in the universe could not make you safer.

And now, I have one more error to try to correct. Among very poor people, among the very poor and uneducated, there is a very popular idea that somehow or other salvation is connected with learning to read and write.

Perhaps you smile, but I know it to be true. I have visited some of them and I will speak to them now.

Often a poor woman has said, "Oh sir! This gospel is no good for poor ignorant creatures like us. There is no hope for me, sir. I cannot read. Do you know, sir, I don't know a letter? I think if I could read a bit I might be saved. But, ignorant as I am, I do not know how to call, because I do not have understanding, sir." I have found this in the country districts as well as in the slums of the city. But virtually all of them could learn to read if they chose to. They could, except they are lazy. And yet they sit down in cold indifference about salvation, with the idea that the pastor can be saved, because he reads so nicely. Or, the store clerk could be saved, for she said, "Amen" so well. Or that the executive could be saved, because he has learned so much and has a great many books in his library. But they could not be saved, because they did not know anything, and that therefore it was impossible.

Now, do I have even one such poor person here? I will speak plainly to you. My poor, uneducated friend, you do not need to know much to go to heaven. I would advise you to know as much as ever you can. Do not be backward in trying to learn. But as far as going to heaven is concerned, the way is so plain that, "those who walk on the way; even if they are fools, they shall not go astray." Do you feel that you have been guilty, that you have broken God's commandments, that you have not kept his Sabbath, that you have taken his name in vain, that you have not loved your neighbor as yourself, nor loved your God with all your heart? Well, if you feel it, Christ died for people like you. He died on the cross, and was punished in your place, and he tells you to believe it.

If you want to hear more about it, come to the house of God and listen, and we will try to instruct you further. But remember, all you need to know to get to heaven is the two things that begin with "S." Sin and Savior. Do you feel your sin? Christ is your Savior. Trust him. Pray to him. And as sure as you are here now, and I am talking to you, you will one day be in heaven. I will tell you two prayers to pray. The first is, pray this prayer, "Lord, show me myself." That is an easy one for you. Lord, show me myself, show me my heart, show me my guilt, show me my danger, Lord, show me myself. And, when you have prayed that prayer, and God has answered it (and remember, he hears prayer); when he has answered it, and shown you yourself, here is another prayer for you, "Lord, show me yourself. Show me your work, your love, your mercy, your cross, your grace." Pray that, and those are the only prayers you need to pray to get to heaven. "Lord, show me myself," and, "Lord show me yourself." You do not need to know much.

You do not need to be able spell to get to heaven, you do not need to be able to speak proper English to get to heaven. The ignorant and unrefined are welcome to the cross of Christ and salvation.

Excuse my taking the time to answer these popular errors. I answer them because they are popular, and popular among some who are here now. Oh men and women hear the word of God once more. "Everyone who calls on the name of the Lord will be saved." The man of eighty, the child of eight, the young man and the single woman, rich, poor, literate, illiterate, the gospel is preached in all of its fullness and freeness to every person under heaven. "Everyone" (and that shuts no one out), "everyone who calls on the name of the Lord will be saved."

Pleading

And now I have nothing to do except to finish with PLEADING. I urge you, I plead with you, in the name of God, believe the message that I have declared to you from God's word. Do not turn away from me because I have put the message simply. Do not reject it because I have chosen to preach it in a way that all can understand. Listen again, "Everyone who calls on the name of the Lord will be saved." I plead with you to believe this. Does it seem difficult to believe? Nothing is too difficult for the Most High.

Do you say, "I have been so guilty, I cannot believe God will save me"? Hear Jehovah speak: "My thoughts are not your thoughts, neither are your ways my ways, declares the LORD. For as the heavens are higher than the earth, so are my ways higher than your ways and my thoughts than your thoughts." Do you say, "I am shut out. Surely, you cannot mean that he would save me?" Listen. Listen, it says, "Everyone." "Everyone" is a great wide door that lets in the biggest sinners. Oh, surely, if it says, "everyone," you are not excluded if you call. That is the point!

Come now. I must plead with you. I will use a few reasons to persuade you to believe this truth. They will be reasons from the Bible. May God bless them to you, sinner. If you call on Christ's name you will be saved. You will be saved because you are *elect*. No person ever called on Christ's name yet who was not elected. The doctrine of election that puzzles many and frightens more, should not do so. If you believe, then you are elect. If you call on the name of Christ, then you are elect. If you feel that you are a sinner and put your trust in Christ, then you are elect.

Now, the elect must be saved, because there is no hellfire reserved for them. God has predestinated them to eternal life, and they will never perish, and no one will snatch them out of Christ's hand. God does not choose someone and then throw him or her away. He does not elect them and then throw them into the pit of hell. Now, you are elect. You could not have called if you had not been elected. Your election is the reason why you called. In view of the fact that you have called, and do call on the name of God, you are God's elect.

Jehovah's desire will be accomplished! It is a supreme decree. Neither death nor hell can ever erase your name from his book. God's chosen must saved. Though earth and hell oppose him, his strong hand will break through their ranks and lead his people through. You are one of these people. You will stand before his throne at last and see his smiling face in glory everlasting, because you are elect.

Here is another reason. If you call on the name of the Lord you will be saved, because *you are redeemed*. Christ bought you, and paid for you. He poured out the hottest of his heart's blood to pay the purchase price. He broke his heart and split it to splinters to buy your soul from the wrath to come. You have been bought. You may not know it yet, but I see the mark of Christ's blood upon you. If you call on his name, even though you have no comfort at this point, yet Christ has called you his own. Ever since that day when he said, "It is finished," Christ has said, "I delight in him, because I have bought him with my blood," and because you are bought you will never perish.

Not one of Jesus' blood-bought ones was ever lost yet. Hell will never be able to rejoice over the damnation of a redeemed soul. The teaching that a person can be bought with Jesus' blood and yet be damned is horrible. It is too satanic for me to believe. I know that what the Savior did he did. If he redeemed, then he did indeed redeem and those who were redeemed by him are positively redeemed from death and hell and wrath. I can never bring my mind to the unrighteous idea that Christ was punished for a person and then that person will be punished again. I never could see how Christ could stand in a man's place and be punished for that man, and yet that person's punishment is carried out a second time on the man himself.

No, if you have called on God's name, that is the proof that Christ paid the ransom demanded. Come, rejoice! If Christ was punished, God's justice cannot demand a double vengeance, first at the bleeding Savior's hands and then again at yours. Come, soul, place your hand on the Savior's head, and say, "Blessed Jesus, you were punished for me." Oh God, I am not afraid of your wrath. When my hand is on the atonement, strike, but you must strike me through your Son. Strike, if you will, but you cannot because you have struck the Savior and you will certainly not strike again for the same offense. What! Did Christ take one tremendous drink in love, and drink my damnation dry, and shall I be damned after that? God forbid! What! Will God be unrighteous, and forget the Redeemer's work for us, and let the Saviors blood be shed in vain?

Not even hell itself has ever given rein to such a thought. It comes only from the men who are traitors to God's truth. Yes, brothers and sisters, if you call on Christ, if you pray, if you believe, you may be quite certain of salvation, because you are redeemed, and the redeemed must not perish.

Shall I give you one more reason? Christ said, "In my Father's house are many rooms." Believe this truth, it must be true. Christ has prepared a home and a crown, from before the foundation of the world, for all of those who believe, and there is a home for you. Come now. Do you think Christ would prepare a home and not bring the occupant there? Will he make crowns and then lose the heads that are to wear them? Again, God forbid! Turn your eye toward heaven. There is a seat there that must be filled and must be filled by you. There is a crown there that must be worn and must be worn by you.

Oh, be of good cheer. Heaven's preparation will not be overdone. He will make room for those who believe. And because he has made that room, those who believe will come there. Oh! I pray to God that I might know that some soul could take hold of this promise! Where are you? Are you standing away from the crowd, or sitting here on the main floor, or in the highest balcony? Are you feeling your sins? Do you shed tears in secret because of them? Do you moan over your iniquities? Oh take his promise: Everyone, sweet everyone, "Everyone who calls on the name of the Lord will be saved."

Call on the name of the Lord! The devil says it is of no use for you to call. You have been a drunk. Tell him it says, "Everyone." "No," says the evil spirit, "it does not apply to you. You have never been to hear a sermon or been in the house of God in over ten years." Tell him it says, "Everyone." "No," says Satan, "remember your sins of even last night and how you have come into this music hall stained with lust." Tell the devil it says, "Everyone." These are all lies from the father of lies. He wants you to believe you can call on God and still be lost. No! Tell him,

"If all the sins that men have done
　　In thought, or word, or deed,
　Since worlds were made or time begun,
　　　Come meet on one poor head,
　　　The blood of Jesus Christ alone
For all this guilt could well atone."

Oh take this to heart. May God's Spirit do this for you! "Everyone who calls on the name of the Lord will be saved."

LIFTING UP THE BRONZE SERPENT

A Sermon Delivered on Lord's Day Morning, October 19, 1879
by C. H. Spurgeon at the Metropolitan Tabernacle, London

Numbers 21:4-9

From Mount Hor they set out by the way to the Red Sea, to go around the land of Edom. And the people became impatient on the way. And the people spoke against God and against Moses, "Why have you brought us up out of Egypt to die in the wilderness? For there is no food and no water, and we loathe this worthless food." Then the LORD sent fiery serpents among the people, and they bit the people, so that many people of Israel died. And the people came to Moses and said, "We have sinned, for we have spoken against the LORD and against you. Pray to the LORD, that he take away the serpents from us." So Moses prayed for the people. And the LORD said to Moses, "Make a fiery serpent and set it on a pole, and everyone who is bitten, when he sees it, shall live." **So Moses made a bronze serpent and set it on a pole. And if a serpent bit anyone, he would look at the bronze serpent and live.**

John 3:1-18

Now there was a man of the Pharisees named Nicodemus, a ruler of the Jews. This man came to Jesus by night and said to him, "Rabbi, we know that you are a teacher come from God, for no one can do these signs that you do unless God is with him." Jesus answered him, "Truly, truly, I say to you, unless one is born again he cannot see the kingdom of God" Nicodemus said to him, "How can a man be born when he is old? Can he enter a second time into his mother's womb and be born?" Jesus answered, "Truly, truly, I say to you, unless one is born of water and the Spirit, he cannot enter the kingdom of God. That which is born of the flesh is flesh, and that which is born of the Spirit is spirit. Do not marvel that I said to you, 'You must be born again.' The wind blows where it wishes, and you hear its sound, but you do not know where it comes from or where it goes. So it is with everyone who is born of the Spirit."

Nicodemus said to him, "How can these things be?" Jesus answered him, "Are you the teacher of Israel and yet you do not understand these things? Truly, truly, I say to you, we speak of what we know, and bear witness to what we have seen, but you do not receive our testimony. If I have told you earthly things and you do not believe, how can you believe if I tell you heavenly things? No one has ascended into heaven except he who descended from heaven, the Son of Man. **And as Moses lifted up the serpent in the wilderness, so must the Son of Man be lifted up, that whoever believes in him may have eternal life.**

"For God so loved the world, that he gave his only Son, that whoever believes in him should not perish but have eternal life. For God did not send his Son into the world to condemn the world, but in order that the world might be saved through him. Whoever believes in him is not condemned, but whoever does not believe is condemned already, because he has not believed in the name of the only Son of God."

Introduction

If you turn to John's gospel you will notice that it begins with a list of types taken from the Holy Scripture. The Bible begins with the creation. God said, "Let there be light." John begins by declaring that Jesus, the eternal Word, "the true light, which enlightens everyone, was coming into the world." Before he closes his first chapter John introduces another type. This is pictured by Abel's sacrifice. When John the Baptist saw Jesus coming to him he said, "Behold the Lamb of God, who takes away the sin of the world!"

Before the first chapter is finished we are reminded of Jacob's ladder when we find our Lord declaring to Nathanael, "Truly, truly, I say to you, you will see heaven opened, and the angels of God, ascending and descending on the Son of Man."

By the time we have reached the third chapter we have come as far as Israel in the wilderness, and we read the joyful words, "And as Moses lifted up the serpent in the wilderness, so must the Son of Man be lifted up, that whoever believes in him may have eternal life." This morning we are going to speak about this act of Moses, so that everyone of us may look at the bronze serpent and find the promise to be true, "everyone who is bitten, when he sees it, shall live." Perhaps some of you who have looked before will receive a fresh benefit from looking again, while some who have never turned their eyes in that direction may look upon the uplifted Savior this morning and be saved from the burning venom of the serpent, which is that deadly poison of sin that now lurks in their nature and breeds death for their souls. May the Holy Spirit make the word effective to that gracious end.

The Person in Mortal Danger

I invite you to consider the subject first by noticing THE PERSON IN MORTAL DANGER. The bronze serpent was made and lifted up for this person. Our text says, "And if a serpent bit anyone, he would look at the bronze serpent and live."

Let us notice first of all that the fiery serpents came among the people because they had despised God's way and God's food. We read, "the people became impatient on the way." It was God's way, he had chosen it for them, and he had chosen it in wisdom and mercy, but they grumbled about it. As an old writer says, "It was a lonesome way and a long-some way" but still it was God's way. Therefore it should not have been hated by them. God's pillar of fire and cloud went before them, and his servants Moses and Aaron led them like a flock. They should have followed cheerfully. Up until now every step of their journey had been mapped out with wisdom. They should have been quite sure that the order to bypass the land of Edom was also given in wisdom and understanding. But, no! They argued with God's way and wanted to have their own way. This is one of the long standing follies of men; they cannot be content to follow the will of the Lord and keep his commands. They prefer to follow their own will and control their own future.

The people also argued about God's food. He gave them the best of the best, for men "ate of the bread of angels," but they called the manna by an insulting name, which in the Hebrew has a sound of contempt about it. They said, "We loathe this worthless food," as if they thought it lacked substance. They wanted food that was more solid, believing it would be better for energy and health. They were discontent with their God and angry about the food he provided for them, even though it excelled any that mortal man has ever eaten before or since.

This is another example of mankind's foolishness. Their hearts refuse to feed on God's word or believe God's truth. They crave for the food of worldly wisdom, "the leeks and garlic" of superstitious tradition, and "the cucumbers" of speculation. They cannot lower their minds to believe the Word of God or to accept truth so simple a child can understand it. Many demand something deeper than the divine, greater than the infinite, and more liberal than free grace. They quarrel with God's way, and with God's food, and so the fiery serpents of evil lusting, pride, and sin come into their midst.

I may be speaking to some who have up to this moment argued with the commands and teachings of the Lord. I would tenderly warn them that their disobedience and attitude will lead to sin and misery. Rebels against God are likely to grow worse and worse. Following the world's fashions and ways of thinking will lead to following the world's immorality and crimes. If we wish for the food of Egypt we will soon feel the serpents of Egypt. The natural result of turning against God is to find serpents attacking us along our way. If we forsake the Lord in spirit or in doctrine, then temptation will lurk in our path and sin will sting our feet.

I ask you to carefully notice who the people were for whom the bronze serpent was specifically lifted up. It was for those who had actually been bitten by the serpents. The Lord sent fiery serpents among them, but the reason the bronze serpent was lifted up was not because the serpents were among them. It was because the serpents had actually poisoned them that led to the providing of a remedy. "Everyone who is bitten, when he sees it, shall live." The only people who looked and benefited from the wonderful cure lifted up in the midst of the camp were those who had been stung by the vipers.

A common belief is that salvation is for good people, salvation is for those who fight against temptation, salvation is for people who are spiritually healthy. God's word is in disagreement with this opinion. God's medicine is for the sick and his healing is for the diseased. The grace of God through the atonement of our Lord Jesus Christ is for people who are really and truly guilty. We do not preach an emotional salvation from imagined guilt. We preach a real and true pardon for actual violations of God's law. Our gospel is not for those who pretend to be sinners, but really think their lives are okay. You who think you have never done anything really wrong, who think you are good deep down and all right, my message is not for you. I am sent to preach Christ to those who are full of sin and worthy of eternal damnation. The serpent of bronze was a cure for those who had been bitten.

What an awful thing it is to be bitten by a serpent! I dare say some of you remember the case of Edward H. Gurling, one of the keepers of the reptiles in the London Zoological Gardens. It happened in October, 1852, and therefore some of you will remember it. This unhappy man was saying farewell to a friend who was going to Austria and according to the custom of many they had drinks together. He drank a considerable amount of gin, and though he probably would have become angry at anyone who said he was drunk, yet his reason and common sense had evidently become overpowered. He returned to his post at the gardens in an excited condition.

A few months before he had seen an exhibition of snake charming and this was on his poor confused mind. He must imitate the Egyptians and play with snakes. First he took a Morocco venom snake out of its cage and put it around his neck. He twisted it about and whirled it all around him. Luckily for him this did not excite the snake enough to bite Mr. Gurling. The assistant keeper cried out, "For God's sake put the snake back," but the foolish man replied, "I am inspired." Putting back the venom snake, he exclaimed, "Now for the cobra."

This deadly serpent was somewhat dormant because of the cold of the previous night. In his reckless condition, this man placed the cobra close to his body until it revived. It glided downward until its head appeared below the back of his vest. He took it by the body, about a foot from its head, and then grabbed it lower down with his other hand, intending to hold it by the tail and swing it around his head. He held it for an instant facing his face and like a flash of lighting the serpent struck him between the eyes. The blood streamed down his face and he called for help, but his companion fled in horror. He told the jury he did not know how long he was gone, because he was bewildered and confused.

When help arrived Gurling was sitting on a chair after having replaced the cobra in its cage. He said, "I am a dead man." They put him in a cab and took him to the hospital. First his speech went. He could only point to his poor throat and moan. Then his vision failed him and lastly his hearing. His pulse gradually sank and in one hour from the time when he had been struck he was a corpse. There was only a little mark on the bridge of his nose, but the poison spread over the body and he was a dead man.

I tell you that story so that you may use it as a parable and learn to never play with sin and also in order to paint a clear picture for you of what it is to be bitten by a serpent. Suppose that Gurling could have been cured by looking at a piece of bronze. Would that not have been good news for him? There was no treatment for that poor foolish man, but there is a remedy for you. Jesus Christ has been lifted up for those who have been bitten by the fiery serpents of sin! He has been lifted up not only for you who are still playing with the serpent, not only for you who have warmed it close to your body, but for you who are actually bitten and mortally wounded. If any person has been bitten and become diseased with sin and feels the deadly venom in his blood, it is for that person that Jesus is lifted up today. You may think yours is an extreme case, but it is for you that sovereign grace provides a remedy.

The bite of the serpent was painful. We are told in the text that these serpents were "fiery serpents." This may refer to their color, but more likely it is a reference to the burning effects of their venom. It heated and inflamed the blood so that every vein became a boiling river, swollen with anguish. In some people that poison of serpents that we call sin has inflamed their minds. They are restless, unhappy and full of fear and agony. They write their own damnation. They are sure that they are lost and refuse talk of hope. You cannot get them to listen to a calm, straightforward message of grace. Sin works such terror in them that they say with Gurling, "I am a dead man." They feel trapped and are, as David says, "like one set loose among the dead, like the slain that lie in the grave, like those whom God remembers no more."

It was for those bitten by the fiery serpents that the bronze serpent was lifted up and it is for those actually poisoned by sin that Jesus is preached. Jesus died for people who are at their wits' end; for those who cannot think straight, for those in turmoil, for those who are already condemned. These are the kind of people for whom the Son of Man was lifted up on the cross. What a comforting thing that we are able to tell you this.

The bite of these serpents was, as I have told you, certain death. The Israelites could have no question about that, because they saw "that many people of Israel died" They saw their own friends die from the snakebite and helped bury them. They knew why they died and were sure that it was because the venom of the fiery serpents was in their veins. There was no way they could think they could be bitten and still live.

Now, we know that many have suffered death as the result of sin. There is no doubt about what sin will do. We are told by the infallible word of God that, "the wages of sin is death," and that, "sin when it is fully grown brings forth death." We also know that this death is endless misery, because the Bible describes the lost as being "thrown into outer darkness," "where their worm does not die and the fire is not quenched." Our Lord speaks of the condemned going away into everlasting punishment, where "there will be weeping and gnashing of teeth."

We should have no doubt about this. Most of those who profess to doubt it are those who are afraid it will happen to them. They know that they are going down to eternal misery themselves and so they try to shut their eyes to their inevitable doom. Alas, that they should find preachers in the pulpit who will flatter them and allow them to indulge their love of sin by telling them what they want to hear. We are not of that line of preachers. We believe in what the Lord has said in all serious fear for your soul. We know the terrors of the Lord and therefore we try to persuade you to escape from them.

But it was for those who had suffered the deadly bite, for those on who the pale face of death had begun to make its mark, for those whose veins were burning with the awful poison of the serpent inside their bodies. It was for them that God said to Moses, "Make a fiery serpent and set it on a pole, and everyone who is bitten, when he sees it, shall live."

The remedy for the poisoning is effective no matter how close to death the victim is. If a person had just been bitten and felt just a little sting, he could look and live. If he had waited for half an hour this would be unfortunate for him. His speech may have failed him and his pulse would be weak, yet if he could only look he would live at once. There was no limit to the effectiveness of the divinely ordained cure or to its availability to all who needed it. The promise had no qualification to it. "Everyone who is bitten, when he sees it, shall live." Our text tells us that God's promise came to pass in every case, without exception. We read, "If a serpent bit anyone, he would look at the bronze serpent and live." I have described for you the person who was in mortal danger.

The Remedy Provided

Next, let us consider THE REMEDY PROVIDED for the person who had been bitten. It was as unusual as it was effective.

It was completely of divine origin. It is clear that the invention of this cure and the power it carried was entirely from God. Men have prescribed various treatments and medications, for snake bites. I do not know how reliable any of them may be, but I know this: I would rather not be bitten in order to try any of them, even the ones that are the most popular at the moment.

There was no remedy in the wilderness for the bites of the fiery serpents, except what God had provided. At first glance, that remedy must have seemed to be a very doubtful one. A simple look at a figure of a serpent on a pole? How unlikely to be successful! How could a cure be accomplished by merely looking at twisted bronze? Indeed, it almost seemed like cruel teasing to tell peope to look at the very thing that had caused their misery. Will the bite of a serpent be cured by looking at a serpent? Will what brings death also bring life? But this is how we know that the remedy came from God.

When God appoints a cure he obligates himself to make it effective. He will not create a plan that fails. He will not ask us to do something to mock us. It should always be enough for us to know God has appointed a way of blessing us. If he ordains it, it must accomplish the promised result. We do not need to know *how* it will work. It is quite enough for us to know that God's mighty grace has promised to make it work for the good of our souls.

This method of curing someone with a serpent lifted on a pole was extremely instructive, even though I suppose that Israel did not understand it. We have the advantage of our Lord's teaching and know the meaning. This bronze serpent was represented as a serpent that had been run through with a sharp pole and then hung up as dead for everyone to see.

It was the image of a dead snake. It is amazing that our Lord Jesus would lower himself to be represented by a dead serpent. The lesson for us to learn after reading John's gospel is this: Our Lord Jesus Christ, in infinite humiliation, lowered himself to come into the world and to be made a curse for us. There was no venom in the bronze serpent, but it was made in the form of a poisonous fiery serpent. Christ is not a sinner and there is no sin in him. But as the bronze serpent was in the form of a serpent, so Jesus was lifted up to God "in the likeness of sinful flesh." He came under the law and "for our sake God made him to be sin." Therefore he came under the wrath and curse of God for us. If you will look upon the cross, you will see Christ Jesus. You will see that sin has been put to death and hung up as a dead serpent. Death has been put to death. Our Savior Christ Jesus has "abolished death and brought life and immortality to light through the gospel." This is where the curse ended forever, because he endured it. Christ became "a curse for us, for it is written, 'Cursed is everyone who is hanged on a tree.'"

The serpents of sin are hung up upon the cross for everyone to see. They have all been slain by our dying Lord. Sin, death, and the curse are like dead serpents now. Oh, what a sight! If you can see it what joy it will give you. If the Israelites had understood what that dead serpent dangling from a pole meant, they would have seen it as a prophecy to them of the glorious sight which we can see today through faith. Jesus was slain; and sin, death, and hell were slain in him. To be healed from the venom by simply looking at the bronze serpent is extremely instructive. Today we understand what it represents.

Only One Remedy Provided

Please remember that in all the camp of Israel there was ONLY ONE REMEDY for the snakebite. It was the bronze serpent and there was only one bronze serpent, not two. Israel was not allowed to make another one. If they had made a second one it would have had no effect. There was one, and only one, and it was lifted high in the center of the camp, so that if any person was bitten by a serpent they could look at it and live. There is one Savior, and only one. "There is no other name under heaven given among men by which we must be saved."

The essence of all grace is in Jesus. "For in him all the fullness of God was pleased to dwell." Christ became cursed for us and ended the curse. Christ was slain by sin and destroyed sin. Christ was bruised on his heel by the old serpent, but broke the serpent's head. It is Christ alone who we must look to if we would live. Oh sinner, look at Jesus on the cross. He is the only remedy for all of the ways sin poisons us.

There was only one healing serpent and it was brilliant and shiny. It was a serpent of bronze and bronze is a shiny metal. It was newly made bronze and therefore not dull. Whenever the sun shone, this bronze serpent flashed in brightness. If God had so ordained, it could have been a serpent of wood or of any other metal. But he commanded that it must be made of bronze so that there would be a brilliance about it.

What brightness there is about our Lord Jesus Christ! If we simply display him in his own true metal he is radiant in the eyes of everyone. If we will only preach the gospel plainly and never try to adorn it with our philosophical opinions, there is enough brightness in Christ to catch a sinner's eye. Indeed, it does catch the eyes of thousands. All the world over, the everlasting gospel gleams in the person of Christ. Just as the bronze serpent reflected the beams of the sun, so Jesus reflects the love of God for sinners, and seeing it they look by faith and live.

The Remedy Is Enduring

Once more, THIS REMEDY WAS AN ENDURING ONE. It was a serpent of bronze and I suppose it remained in the middle of the camp from that day on. There was no use for it after Israel entered the promised land, but, as long as they were in the wilderness, it was probably displayed in the center of the camp, close to the entrance of the tabernacle, on a tall pole. This image of a dead snake was lifted high and available for all to look on. It continued as the cure for serpent venom. If it had been made of other materials it might have been broken or have decayed. But a serpent of bronze would last as long as fiery serpents pestered the wilderness camp.

As long as there was a person bitten there was the serpent of bronze to heal them. What a comfort this is, that Jesus is still "able to save to the uttermost those who draw near to God through him since he always lives to make intercession for them." The dying thief saw the brightness of that serpent of bronze as he saw Jesus hanging at his side, and it saved him! You too may look and live because he is Jesus Christ "the same yesterday and today and forever."

> Faint my head, and sick my heart,
> Wounded, bruised, in every part,
> Satan's fiery sting I feel
> Poisoned with the pride of hell:
> But if at the point to die,
> Upward I direct mine eye,
> Jesus lifted up I see,
> Alive by him who died for me.

I hope I do not cloud my subject with these comparisons. I do not wish to do so. I want to make it very plain to you. All of you who are truly guilty, all of you who are bitten by the serpent, the certain cure for you is to look at Jesus Christ. He took our sin upon him and died in the sinner's place. "For our sake God made him to be sin who knew no sin, so that in him we might become the righteousness of God." Your only remedy is in Christ and nowhere else. Look at him and be saved.

The Application of the Remedy

This brings us to consider THE APPLICATION OF THE REMEDY or the relationship between the person bitten by the snake and the bronze serpent that was to heal them.

What was the connection? It was of the simplest kind imaginable. If God had ordained it, the bronze serpent might have been carried into the sick person's house, but that was not the way. It might have been required that they touch the serpent, or repeat a certain form of prayer, or have a priest present who would perform a ceremony, but there was nothing of the kind. They only needed to look. It was good that the cure was so simple, because the danger was everywhere. Bites of the serpent came in many ways. Someone might be gathering wood for cooking or just be walking along and be bitten. Even today snakes in the desert present a danger. Mr. James

Sibree, the well-known missionary to Madagascar, says that on one occasion he saw what he thought was a round stone with beautiful markings. He stretched out his hand to pick it up, when to his horror he discovered that it was a coiled-up snake.

When the fiery serpents were sent among the Israelites, the danger was constant. There was danger in their beds and at their meals, danger in their houses and when they went outside. Isaiah does not call them "flying fiery serpents" because they actually fly, but because they tense themselves and then suddenly spring up, reaching a considerable height. A man might be wearing knee-high leather boots and still not be safe from these dangerous reptiles. What could someone do if he was bitten? He had nothing to do except stand outside his tent door and look to the place where the brightness of the bronze serpent gleamed. The moment he looked he was healed.

He had nothing to do but to look. No priest was needed, no holy water, no hocus-pocus, no mass book, nothing but a look. A Roman Catholic bishop said to one of the early Reformers who preached salvation by simple faith, "Oh Mr. Doctor, if you offer free salvation to the people we will be out of business." And indeed they are, because the business and trade of priest craft are ended forever if people may simply trust Jesus and live. And yet, this is the case. Believe in him, you sinners, for this is the spiritual meaning of looking. Look and your sin is immediately forgiven. And perhaps more importantly, the deadly power of sin ceases to operate within your spirit. There is life in a look at Jesus. What could be easier than that?

The Remedy Is Personal

But please notice how VERY PERSONAL it was. Nothing anyone else could do for the person would cure them. If they had been bitten by the serpent and refused to look at the serpent of bronze, and just went to his bed, no doctor could help them. A godly mother might kneel down and pray for a child, but it would be of no use. Sisters might come in and plead for it, ministers might be called in to pray for the one to be healed, but if they did not look, they were doomed to die despite their prayers.

There was only one hope for their life. They must look at that serpent of bronze. The situation is the same with you. Some of you have written to me begging me to pray for you and I have. But it is no advantage to you unless you yourselves believe in Jesus Christ. There is no hope on earth or in heaven for any of you unless you will believe in Jesus Christ. Whoever you may be, however severely you have been bitten by the serpent, however close to death you are, if you will look at the Savior, you will live. But if you will not do this you must be damned, as surely as you are alive.

At the last great day I must be a witness against you that I have told you this directly and clearly. "Whoever believes and is baptized will be saved, but whoever does not believe will be condemned." There is no other help for you. You may do what you wish, join whatever church you please, take the Lord's Supper, be baptized, go through severe penances, or give everything you have to feed the poor, but you are a lost person unless you look at Jesus. This is the only remedy. Even Jesus Christ himself cannot, will not, save you unless you look at him. There is nothing in his death to save you, there is nothing in his life to save you, unless you will trust him. The most important thing, the only thing is this, you must look and you must look for yourself.

The Remedy Is Instructive

THIS CURE IS VERY INSTRUCTIVE. This looking, what did it mean? It meant this: Self-help must be abandoned and God must be trusted. The wounded person would say, "I must not sit here and look at my wound. That will not save me. See where the serpent struck me. The blood is oozing out and it is black with the venom! It burns and swells! My very heart is failing. But sitting here thinking about it will not cure me. I must look away from my bite mark and look to the uplifted serpent of bronze."

It is pointless to look anywhere except to God's one appointed remedy. The Israelites must have understood what was required of them. God requires us to trust him and to use his appointed way of salvation. We must do as he tells us and trust in him to work his cure. If we will not do this we will die eternally.

This method of curing was intended to increase their understanding of the love of God and give God's grace the complete credit for the healing. The bronze serpent was not merely a picture, as I have shown you, of God's putting away sin by expending his wrath on his Son; it was a display of divine love. And I know this because Jesus himself said, "And as Moses lifted up the serpent in the wilderness, so must the Son of Man be lifted up." "For God so loved the world that he gave his only Son, that whoever believes in him should not perish but have eternal life."

This clearly says that the death of Christ on the cross was a display of God's love for people. Whoever looks at that greatest display of God's love, namely, his giving his only Son to become a curse for us, will definitely live. When a man was healed by looking at the serpent he could not say that he healed himself. All he did was look and there is no healing power in a look. Believers never claim merit or honor because of their faith. They know their faith did not come from themselves and they never brag about it. What is the great accomplishment in simply believing the truth and humbly trusting Christ to save you? Faith glorifies God and for that reason our Lord has chosen it as the means of our salvation.

If a priest had come and touched the bitten person, then some of the honor for the cure might have gone to him. But when there was no priest involved, when there was nothing except looking at that bronze serpent, the person was driven to the conclusion that God's love and power had healed them. I am not saved by anything that I have done, but by what the Lord has done. God will have us all come to that conclusion. We must confess that if we are saved, it is by his free, rich, sovereign, undeserved grace that he has displayed in the person of his dear Son.

The Cure Accomplished

Allow me one moment on this point, THE CURE ACCOMPLISHED.

We are told in the text that "if a serpent bit anyone, they would look at the bronze serpent and live." That is to say, they were healed immediately. They did not have to wait five minutes, or five seconds. Dear hearer, did you ever hear this before? If you have not, it may surprise you, but it is true. If you have lived in the blackest sin that is possible up to this very moment, yet if you will now believe in Jesus Christ you will be saved before the clock ticks again. It is done like a flash of lightning. Pardon is not a work of time.

Sanctification needs a lifetime, but justification needs no more than a moment. You believe, you live. You trust in Christ, your sins are gone. You are a saved person the instant you believe. "Oh," one says, "that is a wonder." It is a wonder and will remain a wonder for all eternity. Our Lord's miracles, when he was on earth, were mostly instantaneous. He touched them and the fevered ones were able to sit up and minister to him. No doctor can cure a fever in that way. There is a weakness that lingers after the heat of the fever has come to an end. Jesus' cures are perfect. Whoever believes in him, though he has only believed for one minute, is justified from all his sins. Oh the matchless grace of God!

The Remedy Is Continual

THIS REMEDY HEALED AGAIN AND AGAIN. Very possibly after a man had been healed he might go back to his work and be attacked by a second serpent. There were dens of them all around. What was he to do if he was bitten again? Why, to look again. If he was wounded a thousand times he must look a thousand times. Dear child of God, if you have sin on your conscience, look at Jesus. The healthiest way to live where serpents swarm is to never take your eye off the bronze serpent at all. Ah, you vipers, you may bite if you wish. As long as my eye is on the bronze serpent, I defy your fangs and your poison, because I have a constant remedy at work within me. Temptation is overcome by the blood of Jesus. "This is the victory that has overcome the world—our faith."

The Remedy Cures Everyone Who Uses It

THE REMEDY WORKED EVERY TIME it was tried. There was not one case in all the camp of a person who looked at the serpent of bronze and died. And there will never be a case of a person who looks at Jesus and remains condemned by God. The believer must be saved. Some of the people had to look from a long distance. The pole could not be equally close to everyone, but as long as they could see the serpent it healed those who were a long way off as well as those who were close by. It did not matter if their eyesight was weak. Not everyone's eyesight was strong. Some may have had to squint, or their vision was dim, or they had only one eye, but if they only looked they lived.

Perhaps someone could hardly make out the shape of the serpent as he looked. "Ah," he said to himself, "I cannot make out the coils of the bronze snake, but I can see the shining of the bronze," and he lived. Oh, poor soul, if you cannot see all of Christ, not all his beauty, nor all the riches of his grace, yet if you can only see him who was made sin for us you will live. If you say, "Lord, I believe; help my unbelief," your faith will save you. A little faith will give you a great Christ and you will find eternal life in him.

I have tried to describe the cure. Oh that the Lord would work that cure in every sinner here at this moment. I do pray he may.

It is a pleasant thought that if they looked at that bronze serpent in any kind of light they lived. Many saw it in the glare of noon. They saw its shining coils and lived. But I assume that some were bitten at night. By the moonlight they could come close and look up and live. Perhaps it was a dark and stormy night and not a star was visible. The storm crashed overhead and from the dark cloud out flashed the lightning, splitting the rocks apart. By the glare of that sudden flash the dying person could make out the bronze serpent. Though they saw it for only a moment, yet they lived.

So, sinner, if your soul is a raging storm within you, and if from out of the dark cloud there comes only one single flash of light, look to Jesus Christ by it and you will live.

A Lesson for Believers

I close with this last thought. There is A LESSON here for those who love their Lord.

What should we be doing? We should imitate Moses. His job was to set the bronze serpent on a pole. Your job and mine is to lift up the gospel of Christ Jesus, so that everyone may see it. All Moses had to do was to hang up the bronze serpent so everyone could see it. He did not say, "Aaron, bring your censer, and bring other priests, and make a perfumed cloud." Nor did he say, "I myself will go out in my robes as a judge and giver of the law and stand there." No, he had nothing to do that was official or ceremonial. His only job was to display the bronze serpent where everyone could gaze upon it.

He did not say, "Aaron, bring a blanket of gold," or, "wrap up the serpent in blue and scarlet and fine linen." He was to keep the serpent exposed for all to see. Its power lay in itself—not in the way it was decorated. The Lord did not tell him to paint the pole with the colors of the rainbow. Oh, no. Any pole would do. Those who were dying did not need to see the pole. They only needed to see the serpent. I would think Moses made a nice looking pole, because God's work "should be done decently and in order." But still, the serpent was the only thing to look at.

This is what we are to do with our Lord. We must preach *him*, teach *him*, and make *him* visible to everyone. We must not hide him by our attempts at eloquence and learning. We must not use the polished beautiful grain pole of fine speech or the colorful art of grand sentences and poetic passages. Everything must be done so that Christ can be seen. Nothing that hides him must be allowed. Moses could go home and go to bed once the serpent was lifted up. All that was needed was for the bronze serpent to be visible both by day and night. The preacher may hide himself, so that no one will know who he is. If he has presented Christ, he is better off out of the way.

Now you Sunday School teachers, teach your children Jesus. Show them Christ crucified. Keep Christ before them. You young men who try to preach, do not attempt to do it in a grand style. The true greatness of preaching is for Christ to be greatly displayed in it. No other greatness is needed. Keep self in the background, but present Jesus Christ to the people, preach Christ crucified. Only Jesus, only Jesus. Let him be the heart and most important part of all of your teaching.

I know some of you have looked at the bronze serpent and been healed. But what have you done with the bronze serpent since then? You have not come forward to confess your faith and join the church. You have not spoken to anyone about their soul. You have put the bronze serpent into a chest and hidden it away. Is this right? Bring it out and set it on a pole. Proclaim Christ and his salvation. He was never meant to be treated like a curiosity in a museum. He is to be displayed where anyone who has been bitten by sin may look at him.

"But, I do not have a good pole," someone says. The best kind of pole to show Christ on is a high one, so that he may be seen from great distances. Exalt Jesus. Speak well of his name. I do not know what other good there can be in the pole except its height. The more you can speak to your Lord's praise, the higher you can lift him up, the better. Talking about religion does not help. Lift Christ up. "Oh," says another, "but I do not have a long pole." Then lift him up on the pole that you do have. There are short people around who will be able to see Christ as you lift him up.

I think I told you once about a picture that I saw of the bronze serpent. I want the Sunday School teachers to listen to this. The artist represented all kinds of people crowded around the pole, and as they looked the horrible snakes dropped off their arms, and they lived. There were so many people around the pole that a mother could not get close to it. She carried a little baby, who a serpent had bitten. You could see the blue marks of the venom. Since she could not get close enough for the baby to see, the mother held her child high into the air, and turned his little head so that he could gaze with his infant eye on the bronze serpent and live. Sunday School teachers, do this with your little children. Even while they are still little, pray that they will look at Jesus Christ and live. There is no limit at what age they may be saved.

Old men bitten by snakes came hobbling on their crutches. "I am eighty years old," one says, "but I have looked at the bronze serpent and I am healed." Little boys were brought out by their mothers, and even though they were not old enough to speak plainly, they cried in their childish language, "I look at the great snake and it bless me." All classes, and genders, and characters, and temperaments looked and lived.

Who will look at Jesus at this hour? Oh dear souls, will you have life or not? Will you despise Christ and perish? If so, your blood is on your own conscience. I have told you God's way of salvation. Seize it. Look at Jesus right now. May his Spirit gently lead you to do so. Amen.

A Poor Man's Prayer

A Sermon Delivered
by C. H. Spurgeon at the Metropolitan Tabernacle, London

Psalm 106:4-5

Remember me, O LORD, when you show favor to your people,
    help me when you save them.
    (Or, help me with your salvation.)
that I may look upon the prosperity of your chosen ones,
    that I may rejoice in the gladness of your nation,
    that I may glory with your inheritance.

Introduction

Beloved, we always consider it a very hopeful sign when a person begins to take religion personally. To simply come with the crowd and go through the motions of worship is poor work. But when a person gets to feeling the weight of their own sin and confesses it with their heart before God, when they want a Savior for themself and begin to pray alone asking that they may find that Savior, when they are not content with being the child of godly parents or with having attended church since early childhood, when they hunger for real godliness, personal religion, and true conversion; it is a happy sign.

When a buck separates from the herd we assume it has been shot, the wound is serious, and the creature is seeking solitude. A bleeding heart does not want company. Blessed are the wounds God inflicts, because they lead to a heavenly healing!

We are even gladder when this desire for personal salvation leads a person to pray. When someone really begins to cry out before God of their own volition, when they quit using the prayers they used to repeat like a parrot, and burst out with the language of the heart, then we have high hope. Even though the language may be very broken or consist of only sighs and tears and groans, it is a happy sign. "Behold, he is praying" was enough to convince Ananias that Paul was converted.

When we find someone praying, and praying earnestly, for personal salvation, we feel that this is the finger of God, and our heart is glad.

The passage before us is one of those earnest personal prayers that we love to hear from any lips. I will read it again and then proceed to use it in two or three ways. "Remember me, O LORD, when you show favor to your people, help me with your salvation, that I may look upon the prosperity of your chosen ones, that I may rejoice in the gladness of your nation, that I may glory with your inheritance."

First, this is a very suitable prayer for the humble believer. It was a humble believer who first spoke these words. Next, it would make a very suitable prayer for a repentant backslider. And finally, it would be a very sweet gospel prayer for a seeker. May the Spirit of God bless the word to people in each of these situations.

A Suitable Prayer for a Humble Christian

First, then, this is A VERY PROPER PRAYER FOR A DOWNCAST HUMBLE CHRISTIAN. I think I can hear the Psalmist using these very words.

Notice the first fear this poor trembling Christian feels. He is afraid that he is so insignificant that God will forget him. And so he begins with, "Remember me, O LORD, when you show favor to your people," I know this man well. I think about him very often, but he thinks very little about himself. I admire his humility, but he often complains that he feels pride in his heart. He is a true believer, but he is a sad doubter. Poor man. He often hangs his head, because he has such a sense of his own unworthiness. I only wish he had an equal sense of Christ's fullness to balance his humility.

He is on the road to heaven, but he is often afraid that he is not and that makes him watch every step he takes. I almost wish some confident professors of Christianity doubted like our humble brother. They would be closer to the kingdom if they were only half as cautious as he is. He is afraid to put one foot in front of another because he might take a wrong step. And yet he regrets he is not careful enough. He is always complaining about the hardness of his heart and yet he is tenderness itself.

Dear man. You should hear him pray. His prayers are among the most earnest and blessed you ever listened to, but when he has finished he is afraid he should never have opened his mouth. He says he is not qualified to pray in front of others. He thinks his prayers are the worst that ever reach the throne of God. He is afraid they do not get there, that his words are only so much wasted breath. He does have occasional moments of sunshine. There are times when he has a ray of hope, when he feels the love of God in his soul, and he is as happy as the cricket on the hearth in Charles Dickens' fairy tale. There is not a man outside of heaven more carefree than he is when his hope revives.

But, oh, he has such a tender conscience about sin that when he finds himself growing a little cold, or backsliding in the slightest degree, he begins to torture himself. I am glad he is so sensitive about sinning, but he also begins to doubt his Lord's care for him, and about that I am not glad. We pity him and blame him at the same time. Now, I am not quite certain about this good man's name. Could it be John Bunyan's Little-Faith, or Feeble-Mind? Or is it Mr. Despondency I am thinking of? Or am I speaking about Miss Much-Afraid Or is it Mr. Ready-to-Halt? Well, it is someone in that numerous family. This poor soul thinks, "Surely God will forget me!" No, no, dear heart, he will not forget you.

It is wonderful how God does think of little things. Mungo Park, the Scottish explorer of Africa who died at an early age in 1806, tells the story of picking up a little bit of moss in the desert. As he noticed how beautiful and colorful it was, he said, "God is here. He is thinking of the moss and therefore he will think of me."

The story is told of a little plant that grew in the middle of the forest. The trees stretched for miles around and the little plant said to itself, "The sunlight will never get to me. I have a little flower within me that I would gladly open, but it cannot blossom until the sunbeams care for me. Alas! they will never reach me. Look at the branches with their leaves. See the huge trunks of those towering oaks and mighty beeches. They will hide the sun from such a tiny plant." But in due season the sun looked through the trees like a king through the window of his castle and smiled on the little flower, because there has never been a flower that God has not thought about and provided for. The saying, "each blade of grass has its own drop of dew," is true. Do you think that God will forget you, little as you are? He knows when swallows fly, and when ants awaken and gather their food, and will he not think of you?

You must not suspect the love of your heavenly Father because you are little in your own eyes. Mother, which child is the one you will never forget? If you ever went to bcd at night and left one of the children outside, I know which one it was not. It was not the baby who lies helpless in your arms. Your never forget that one. And you helpless ones, you timid trembling ones, if the Lord must forget any, it would be the strong, but certainly not you. As you breathe the prayer, "Remember me, O LORD, when you show favor to your people," the Lord answers you, "I do remember you still."

Next, notice that this poor trembling heart seems to be in great trouble because he is afraid the Lord will pass him by. At the same time, he feels that every good thing he can possibly receive must come from the Lord. Notice the words, "Remember me, O Lord, when you show favor to your people, help me with your salvation." It is as if he said, "Lord, I cannot come to you. I am too crippled to come, I am too weak to come, but help me. Oh Lord, I am like the wounded man who fell among robbers on his way from Jerusalem to Jericho. I am half dead and cannot help myself. Come to me, Lord, because I cannot come to you. Visit me, because only your visit can give me life. I am so wounded, and broken, and incomplete, that if you do not visit me with your salvation, I must be lost. Visit me with your salvation as if I have never been saved before!"

Now, poor trembling one, let me whisper a word in your ear. May the Holy Spirit give you comfort with it. If you have a broken heart, you do not need to say, "Lord, help me." Do you not know that he lives in you? Is it not written, "This is the one to whom I will look; he who is humble and contrite in spirit and trembles at my word"? Are you not that very person? I wish you could rejoice at God's word, but since you cannot, I am glad you tremble at it. You are the one with whom God has promised to live. "Trembles at my word." Take hold of that. Believe that the Lord looks in your direction and is with you.

"Remember me, O Lord." What a sad prayer this is! This poor, weak, humble, trembling person wants to join in the blessings that the Lord gives to his own people. He wants to take part in the joy the Lord has prepared for them. This is the way he talks. "I hear many Christians around me say that they know and are persuaded that they are the Lord's. I wish I had a little of their assurance. I hear them speak so confidently. I see the light leap out of their eyes when they talk about their sweet Lord and Master, and all his love for them. Oh, how I wish I could talk like that! Poor me. I am only able to say, 'Lord, I believe, help my unbelief.'

"I see them sitting at a table loaded with wonderful things and they seem to enjoy the large quantities set before them. But as for me, I am glad it is written that, 'even the dogs under the table eat the children's crumbs.' If I get a crumb now and then, I feel so happy with it. But I wish I could sit and feast where others of God's children do. Oh that I could experience happy fellowship, and closeness, and inward joy, and overflowing delight. Some of them tell me that they sit down on the doorstep of heaven, and look inside and see the streets of gold, and sometimes hear the stray notes from the harps of the blessed ones in the far-off country. Oh, how I wish I had a sip of these joys, but 'Woe is me, that I sojourn in Meshech, that I dwell among the tents of Kedar!' The only music I hear is the unpleasant noise of a sinful world, the stringed instruments of those who enjoy immoral songs. I miss having those precious things in which the saints delight."

Poor sorrowing heart. Let me say to you, and say it in God's name, if you love your Lord, all things are yours. They are yours to freely enjoy even at this moment. The Lord will not deny you any covenant blessing. Be bold to ask for and receive these holy joys. It does not matter if you are the least child in the family The inheritance of each of God's children is the same. God will not deny you anything that he would give to any of his other children. In fact, if there is one morsel tastier than another, it is reserved for people like you. Be bold! If you are like Benjamin, who was not admired by his stepbrothers, then your greater brother Joseph will fill your plate ten times higher than theirs. The Lord will comfort and bless you. Only be of good cheer. When you are praying, "Remember me, O Lord, when you show favor to your people," let your faith hear him reply, "I am your portion and your inheritance." Rejoice in the Lord your God. "Lift your drooping hands and strengthen your weak knees." Is not my text a sweet prayer for you? Pray it in faith and be at peace.

A Suitable Prayer for a Repentant Backslider

We will now look at the text in another way. Our text is AN APPROPRIATE PRAYER FOR A POOR REPENTANT BACKSLIDER. I know there are backsliders here, although I regret to say I am not sure that they truly regret their behavior. Only the Lord can read their hearts. But if they truly are sorry, I can hardly think of a better prayer for them than this, "Remember me, O Lord, when you show favor to your people,"

It is obvious that this poor, praying backslider feels that he has forgotten his God. Have you done that? Have you been a church member and gone sadly astray? Have you completely forgotten his commandments? You thought you loved him. You used to pray once. You enjoyed reading the Bible and hearing the Word preached. But now you find your pleasure somewhere else. You have left your first love and gone after many lovers. But now you are sorry you forgot about him. You wish the Lord would be gracious to you once again even though you have ignored him. The prayer leaps to your lips. "Remember me, O Lord." Blessed be his name. He does not forget us like we so easily forget him.

If you are a truly penitent backslider, your feelings of repentance prove that God remembers you. If God had really completely forgotten about you, then you would not have any desire to return to him. Those intense emotions, those secret struggles, those desires to be restored to the Lord; these prove that he remembers you with the favor he has toward his people.

And, then, I think your next trouble will be this: You feel that you have lost your fellowship with Christ. You are right in feeling this way. How can two walk together unless they are in agreement? How could Christ have fellowship with you while you enjoy your foolish ways? Do you think Christ would come and have a friendly conversation with you while you are acting so thoughtlessly, or while you are so impure? How could that be? You have broken all happy fellowship between your soul and God. You are right to pray, "Remember me, O Lord; help me when you save your people. Come and live in me again. Why should my foolish passions wander? Where can I find such sweetness like I have tasted in your love? Where can I find love like the love you have for me? Come back, my Lord, and visit me with your salvation." Is this not a prayer made just for you?

Next, notice in the text that the poor backslider is longing to get a glimpse of the good things that have been hidden from him for so long. He cries, "That I may look upon the prosperity of your chosen ones." Like the Prodigal Son, he has been out among the pigs, but he could not fill his stomach with the husks they ate. He was dying of hunger and thirst, and now he remembers that his Father's servants have more than enough bread. Backslider, do you remember that tonight? You know you are not happy. You have begun to understand that you never will be happy while you are living in the far country, away from your Father.

If you had not been a child of God you might have been happy in the world; enjoying the kind of happiness the world takes pleasure in. But if you have ever known the love of God, you cannot truly love the things the world does. If you can, then you really have been a hypocrite all along. Do you not sigh to the Lord, hoping he will give you these good things again? Well, he will give them to you freely and he will not scold you. Come and try him. He is ready to embrace you, and to forget and forgive the past, and accept you as his precious child.

The poor backslider, using the words of our text in his prayer, wants to taste again the joy he used to feel. Therefore he says, "That I may rejoice in the gladness of your nation." He wants to be able to say as he was able to before, "That I may glory with your inheritance." Poor man, he is ashamed to speak to sinners now. He hangs his head in their company, because there are some who call him a traitor. He does not like to have it known that he was once a Christian. He sneaks in to the church services as if he hoped no one would notice him. There he is, but he feels half ashamed to be here. And yet he wishes he could be with the Christian fellowship again and rejoice with fellow believers.

My poor friend. You used to be as bold as a lion in your witness for Christ, but now you turn tail and run. How can you be bold with all those inconsistencies? There was a time when you were brave enough to be a martyr, but now what a coward you are. Who could be surprised at your change when they know that secret sin has damaged your profession and made you weak as a kitten? I urge you to pray this prayer: "That I may glory with your inheritance." You will never again be able to boast in the Lord until you are restored. You must return to the day you first cried out, "Father, I have sinned against heaven and before you. I am no longer worthy to be called your son." My brother, my sister, come back even now and receive another application of the blood of Christ. Look to Jesus again.

And may I add here, if you have not backslidden, look again to Jesus. Those of us who have not fallen had better look to him along with our fellow believers who have fallen. We all need the same blessing. We have all wandered to some degree. Come, let us look again at those dear wounds of the Savior. Can you not see him? I see him hanging on the cross now. The crown of thorns is on his head. His eyes are full of pity and deep sorrow. I see his face stained with spittle, and black and blue with cruel bruises. I see his hands butchered by the nails. I see his feet, they gush with streams of crimson blood. I look on him and I cry, "Was ever grief like yours, oh King of sorrow?" And as I look, I remember that "the Lord has laid on him the iniquity of us all." As I look, my sin leaves me, because it was laid on him. I continue looking and my heart begins to love again and then it leaps with joy. I come back to where I once stood and now, once again, Christ is my all, and I rejoice in him. Have you gone through that process, backslider? If you have done this while I have been speaking, let us praise God together.

A Sweet Prayer for a Poor Discouraged Seeker

I hope my last point from this text will be helpful to many who are present here. It is this: This is A VERY SWEET PRAYER FOR A POOR GRIEVING SEEKER. I ask everyone who desires to be converted to remember this prayer. It would be an excellent idea to write it down and carry it home with you. Better yet, whisper this prayer to heaven right now.

Consider it well. In the first place, it is a sinner's prayer. "Remember me, O Lord." I say this, because the dying thief rejoiced to use these words. The poor man was dying. He could not have reached down from the cross for a Prayerbook and read a short prayer. This prayer is the best of prayers. "Jesus, remember me when you come into your kingdom." Trembling sinner, what was good for the dying thief may also be a good prayer for you. Use it now, "Forget my sins, my Father, but remember me. Forget my delays in coming to you, forget how many times I have rejected the Savior, forget the hardness of my heart. But, oh, remember me. Let all my sins die out in your thinking and erase them from your memory. But, dear Father, by the love of the Lord Jesus, do remember me." Sinner, do not go home without breathing this prayer to God.

Notice, again, it is the prayer of someone who is lost. "Help me with your salvation." No one wants salvation unless they are lost. People who do not believe they are lost may talk about salvation, but they do not know anything about it, and they really do not want to. Lost soul, where do you stand? Are you lost in a thousand ways? Are you lost even in your own social group? Well, here is a prayer just for you. "Help me when you save your people." Jesus Christ has not come to seek and to save those who do not want saving. He has come on purpose "to seek and to save the lost." You are the person he came to bless. Look to him and you will find that he is the Savior you need. "Help me with your salvation." I cannot get this prayer into your hearts, but God can. I am praying in my own soul that many of you may be pleading right now, "Help me with your salvation."

Next, notice that our text is the prayer of someone who has trouble seeing. "Help me, that I may *look* upon the prosperity of your chosen ones." We have told seekers to look to Jesus, but they complain, "We do try to look, but we cannot see." Beloved seekers, I do not know that you are asked to *see*. You are asked to *look*; and if you could not see when you looked you would have at least obeyed the gospel command. The *looking*, the *looking* would bring salvation to you. Christ is the great cure for spiritual blindness. Pray right now, "Lord, open my blind eyes, and help me to look upon the prosperity of your chosen ones."

Our text is also a prayer for a heavy heart. "That I may rejoice in the gladness of your nation." The seeking soul groans, "Oh that I had a little joy or even a trembling hope. I would be glad to have even a small bit of understanding." Pray for joy. The Lord waits to give it and if you believe in Jesus your joy will be full.

And in the last place; do not wait until you are too emotionally exhausted to act. Our text is the prayer of someone who is humble and has been brought very low. He asks God to make him able to rejoice with the Lord's people.

He knows there is nothing in him to glory in or brag about. His cry is, "Lord, let me brag about your mercy and your goodness. I have nothing else to brag about."

Now, beloved hearer, I would most seriously encourage you to use this prayer and do it for the following reasons.

Just think for a moment. Assume you are now living without seeing the prosperity of God's chosen ones, that you are not saved. What an unhappy way to live! I cannot understand how a person can live without God. I cannot comprehend how they live. Do you not have things that bother you? "Oh, yes," you say. "I have loads of anxieties." Well, where do you take them? I have plenty of troubles, but I have a God to take them to. What do you do with so many troubles and no God? Do your children never give you stress? How can you live with bad children and no God? Do you never have money problems? Do you never feel distracted? Do you never say, "What shall I do? Where do I turn?" I assume you do.

What do you do without a help or a guide? Poor weak thing that I am, I run under the shelter of my Father's wing and I feel safe enough. But where do you go? Who do you run to? Where do you find comfort? I suppose you might be something like the poor creatures that were condemned to death in olden times. They were given something to drink that would dull their senses, so they could die without feeling the horror of death. Do you fill your life with things so you can live a strong delusion, and believe what is false? If you were in your right mind, you could not live without God. You who have beautiful gardens and fine homes, and wealth and riches, they cannot give you comfort. You who work long hard hours and have little to show for it and are without God, how do you keep your spirits up?

What comfort is there in your life? What are your days like without prayer in the morning? What are your nights like without prayer in the evening? Oh people, I could just as easily live without eating or live without breathing, as live without prayer. Poor soul, how unhappy and miserable you must be with no God to comfort you!

But if it is bad to *live* without Christ, and I am sure it is, what will it be to *die* without him? What will it be to look into the future and find no light? No light and no one who can bring you any? You have sent for the minister, and he has spoken with you, but he cannot help you. Your family prays for you, they cry at the thought of losing you, but you are alone. Your life is like an angry sea in a cold winter storm. Everything is darkness. Or, to change the figure of speech, you are like a man on a sinking ship. He clings to the mast for dear life. The wind blasts past him and immediately comes roaring back around him, as if hungry for its prey. He hears the seagulls screaming in the sky and they seem to be prophesying his doom. The waves break over him, he is drenched by the cold seawater, until he is ready to freeze as he hangs between death's awful jaws. The last lifeboat has carried off all it can and it will never come back. He clings with desperation, but he knows it is hopeless. He will drift out to sea. His corpse will lie at the bottom of the ocean, in the caverns where many thousands of skeletons have come before him. His case is terrible to the nth degree, and yet it is a poor picture of a soul that leaves the body without an interest in Christ's salvation. Cry to God before you reach that point. "Remember me, O Lord, when you show favor to your people; help me when you save them."

But the night is darker and the storm rages with ten times the fury when we come to think what it must be to rise again from the tomb without Christ. When that last shrill trumpet sounds, and every grave and cemetery has given up their sleepers, and the sea has delivered up the dead who are in it, and the battlefields are swarming with the countless slain who live again, and the great white throne is seen in the sky, and the Son of Man who bled for sinners is sitting on it to judge and condemn his enemies; what will people who have no personal religion do then? What will those who have no interest in Christ and no part in his salvation do then?

The Scriptures tell us that they will ask the rocks to hide them and the hills to cover them. But the rocks and the hills have no hearts of compassion. They will offer no protection from God's anger. There will be no shelter for the ungodly. There will be nothing between them and the fiery displeasure and wrath of God. "As I live, declares the Lord GOD, I have no pleasure in the death of the wicked, but that the wicked turn from his way and live; turn back, turn back, from your evil ways, for why will you die?"

Many of you, in this great gathering in the Tabernacle know what I am talking about. This is not the first time I have painted this picture for you. My emotions almost get the best of me even though I see you twice every Sunday. You are all here, and here I am, a lone man, standing here to talk to you in God's name. My soul demands that I am earnest with you, but ah, I do not feel I am half as earnest as I should be. Yet, listen to me once more. I speak to you at this hour like a true prophet as I warn you that if you reject the Savior, you will see this sight again. Only then you will look across the real flames of hell and will say to yourself, "The preacher did warn us. He did tell us to cry to God for mercy. He did point us to the Savior. He told us to pray and pray right then and there."

You will remember my pleas and then your agony will be even greater. You will wail in a pain that will never end. You will cry, "God called, but I refused. He stretched out his hands, but I paid no attention to him. The day of grace has past and the Christ whom I despised laughs at my affliction. My time came and went and now there is no hope, no hope. I knocked at mercy's door too late. My lamp went out like those of the foolish virgins and now I am shut out in outer darkness, where there is weeping and wailing and gnashing of teeth."

In the name of the everlasting God I urge you, I plead with you, submit yourselves to Christ your Lord right now and you will live. Amen. Amen.

KNOCK

A Sermon Delivered on Sunday Morning, May 27, 1883
by C. H. Spurgeon at the Metropolitan Tabernacle, London

Matthew 7:6-11

"Do not give dogs what is holy, and do not throw your pearls before pigs, lest they trample them underfoot and turn to attack you.

"Ask, and it will be given to you; seek, and you will find; **knock, and it will be opened to you**. For everyone who asks receives, and the one who seeks finds, and to the one who knocks it will be opened. Or which one of you, if his son asks him for bread, will give him a stone? Or if he asks for a fish, will give him a serpent? If you then, who are evil, know how to give good gifts to your children, how much more will your Father who is in heaven give good things to those who ask him!"

Introduction

I have no doubt that, strictly speaking, the three actions encouraged in this verse (which are actually one) were intended first and foremost for God's believing people. The Lord said to his disciples, "Do not throw your pearls before pigs." Perhaps some of them who were poor in spirit might turn around and say, "Lord, we are not wealthy. We are too poor to have such a huge treasure of your grace. You have told us not to give what is holy to dogs, but holiness is more something for which we seek than possess."

"Well," says the Lord, "all you need to do is ask and you will have. You do not have because you do not ask. If you will only seek, you will be sure to find. Holy things are like rare pearls. They are waiting to be discovered if you look for them. You only need to knock and spiritual secrets will be open to you, even the deepest truth of God."

Ask. Seek. Knock. Each is a prayer our Lord encourages us to use. Beloved, let us overflow with prayer. Count on this. If we fail to pray, we will undermine the foundation of our peace and sap the strength of our confidence. However, if we continually plead with God, we will grow strong in the Lord. We will be happy in his love and become a blessing to those around us. Do I need to recommend that you spend time with God? Surely, prayer must give you such joy and have become so necessary in your life that I do not need to urge you to pray. Surely, prayer has become such a part of your life that I hardly need to tell you it is your duty or invite you to pray because it is your privilege to do so. Yet I am doing so, because the Master tells you to three times over. A threefold cord is not easily broken. Do not neglect our Lord's words. I urge you to continue in prayer, to include variety in your praying, and to increase the intensity of your devotion. Ask! Seek! Knock! Do not stop asking until you receive. Do not stop seeking until you find. Do not stop knocking until the door is opened to you.

There appears to be a progression in these three actions. Each is the same thought in a different form and each has more force than the previous one. Ask. That is, in the quiet of your spirit, speak with God about your need, and humbly beg him to grant your desires. This is a good and acceptable way to pray.

However, if merely asking does not appear to be succeeding, the Lord wants to awaken you to the need to focus more and desire more before he answers. Let your desires prompt you to Seek. Call in the help of studying God's word, of meditating on it, and applying it practically. Seek for the blessings like those who seek for hidden treasures. These good things are stored up and they are available for passionate people. Discover how you can reach them. Study the promises of God. Read his word carefully. Meditate on his word and salvation thoroughly. These are the means of grace that may bring you the desired blessing. Advance from asking to seeking.

If you have done all this and it still seems that you have not obtained your desire, then Knock. This is more difficult and more painful work. You must knock by using not only your voice, but your whole soul. Push yourself to godliness to reach the blessing. Make every effort to win that for which you are seeking. Asking is a form of living for God. Seeking is a higher form. Knocking is a total dependence on God. God will often give to his people when they keep his commandments what he denies them if they walk carelessly. Remember the words of the Lord Jesus, He said, "If you abide in me, and my words abide in you, ask whatever you wish, and it will be done for you." Holiness is necessary for power in prayer. The life must knock while the lips ask and the heart seeks.

I will change my line of reasoning and say: Ask like a beggar pleading for a handout. They say that begging is a poor trade. But when you use it well with God, no other trade is as profitable. You can get more from God by asking, than by working and not praying. I do strongly recommend that you work for a living, but I even more strongly recommend that you pray. Nothing under heaven pays like persistent prayer. The person who has power in prayer has everything for which they could wish.

Ask like a poor beggar who is hungry and pleads for food. Seek like a merchant who is hunting for valuable pearls, looking everywhere, anxious to give all that he has so that he can obtain a matchless treasure. Seek like a servant who looks carefully after his master's interests and works hard to see him succeed. Seek diligently and add to the earnestness of the beggar the careful watchfulness of the jeweler who is seeking for a precious gem.

If necessary, knock at mercy's door like a lost traveler who is caught out on a cold night in a blinding snowstorm would knock for shelter to keep from dying in the blizzard.

When you have reached the narrow gate of salvation, ask to be admitted by the great love of God. Then look carefully to find the way in and seek to enter in. If the door seems to be shut against you, knock very hard and continue knocking until the door is opened and you are safely inside the home of love.

Once again, ask for what you need, seek for what you have lost, and knock for what has been refused to you. Perhaps this last way of putting it is the best way of illustrating the shades of meaning and the distinctions of these three words. Ask for everything you need; whatever it may be. It is promised to the sincere asker and is therefore a right and good thing to do. Seek for what you have lost; for what Adam lost for you by the Fall, for what you have lost yourself by your neglect, by your backsliding, and by your lack of prayer. Keep seeking until you find the grace you need. Then knock. If the door to comfort, to knowledge, to hope, to God, to heaven, seems locked against you, then knock, because the Lord will open to you. Only Jesus can open the door for you. You can ask and receive, you can seek and find, but you cannot knock and open. The Lord himself must open the door or you are shut out forever. God is ready to open the door. Remember, there is no angel with a flaming sword to guard this gate. The Lord Jesus himself opens and no one will shut. But I must close this line of thought now, because my desire is to use our text to speak to those who are not yet saved.

Last Sunday, we preached on the glory that awaited God's pilgrims at the end of life's journey. It was a very, very happy time. We reached the suburbs of the Celestial City and we tasted eternal glory. This morning I thought we would begin at the beginning, and enter in at the wicket-gate, that stands at the start of the way to heaven. John Bunyan, in his *Pilgrim's Progress*, says,

"Now over the gate there was written, 'Knock, and it will be opened to you.'" His imaginative allegory is always as truthfully educational as it is delightfully entertaining. I decided that these words Bunyan had over the gate would be my text today. If it is considered worthy to be written over the gate that leads to eternal life, then it must demand the close attention of those who have not yet started on the road to glory, but are anxious to do so. May God the Holy Spirit instruct and stir them while we listen to the Lord from inside the door to his palace saying, "Knock, and it will be opened to you."

The Door of Mercy May Appear to Be Locked

First, then, dear friend, whoever you are, if you are truly anxious to enter into eternal life, I would explain the words over the gate to you, by first saying, THE DOOR OF MERCY MAY APPEAR TO BE LOCKED AGAINST YOU. It is implied in the text: "Knock, and it will be opened to you." If you thought the door stood wide open, there would be no reason for knocking. But because you are uneasy and think it has been locked against you, it is your job to seek to gain entrance by knocking.

To a large extent this uneasiness is the result of your own fears. You think the gate is closed and locked to you, because you think it should be. You feel that if God dealt with you like you would deal with others he would be so offended with you that he would shut the door of his favor against you once and for all. You remember how guilty you have been, how often you have refused God's call, and how you have gone on from evil to evil, and therefore you fear that the Master of the house has already gotten up and shut the door. You are afraid that you are like the stubborn people in Noah's day who came to the ark too late and found the door tightly closed against them. You fear that you have also come too late and will perish in the general destruction.

Your sin stands at the door and blocks it. Your discouragement makes you think the gate of grace is locked to you. But, it is not! The gate is not barred and bolted like you think it is. The Bible does talk about the door being closed in a certain sense, yet in another sense it is never shut. In any case it opens quite freely. Its hinges are not rusted and no bolts secure it. The Lord is glad to open the gate to every knocking soul. It is closed far more in your imagination than it is in fact. As far as the believing sinner is concerned, the sin that shuts it is removed. If you had enough faith, you could enter in at this very moment. And once inside you would never be put out again, because it is written, "Whoever comes to me I will never cast out." If you could abandon your fears and, with holy courage, authorize yourself to come in, you would never be blamed for it. Fear and shame stand in the sinner's way and push him back. Blessed is he whose desperate need forces him to be bold.

One thing we should remember when we are afraid that the door is closed against us, is that it is not as tightly closed as the door of our heart has been. There is a famous painting titled, The Light of the World. It seems to me to be one of the finest sermons the eye has ever looked upon. There stands the ever blessed Lord Jesus, lantern in one hand and knocking at the door of the soul with the other. But the hinges are rusted, the door is firmly bolted, and wild briars and all kinds of creeping plants run up the door to prove that it has been a long time since it was opened. You know what it all means. Continuing in sin has made it harder to open to Christ's knock. Evil habits have crept in one after another until the soul is so firmly bound that it cannot open to the sacred knocking.

Jesus has been knocking at some of your hearts ever since you were children; and he still knocks. I hear his blessed hand knocking on the door at this moment. Do you hear it? Will you open the door of your soul? Jesus has knocked for a long time and still he knocks again. I am sure that you have not knocked at mercy's door for as long as Jesus in his mercy has waited at your door. You know you have not. So, how can you complain if there seems to be a delay in answering your prayers? It is only to make you feel a holy shame for treating your Lord so badly. Now you begin to know what it is to be kept waiting, what it is to grow tired of knocking, what it is for your Beloved to cry "my head is wet with dew, my locks with the drops of the night." This should motivate you to repent for your unkind behavior and also move you to love that gentle Lover of your soul, who has shown such patience toward you, more intensely than ever. It will be no loss to you that the door was shut for a while, if you gain a remorseful heart and a tender spirit.

However, let me warn you that the door can be closed and kept shut by unbelief. The person who believes enters into Christ when he or she believes. The person who enters in by the door will be saved and will go in and out and find pasture. Our Lord tells us this in the tenth chapter of John's gospel. John also tells us, "Whoever believes in the Son has eternal life." There is no question about that. But on the other hand, we also read in the book of Hebrews, "They were unable to enter because of unbelief." The tribes of Israel were in the wilderness, going toward Canaan for forty years, and yet they never reached the promised land because of unbelief. And what if some of you should hear the gospel for forty years? You come and you go, you come and you go, you hear sermons, you watch baptisms and the celebration of the Lord's Supper, you join God's people in worship. What if, after all those forty years, you should never enter because of unbelief? Souls, I tell you, if each one of you lived as long as Methuselah, you could not enter in unless you believed in Jesus Christ. The moment you have trusted him with your whole heart and soul you are inside the entrance of the Father's house. But however many years you may be asking, seeking, and knocking, you will never enter in until faith comes, because unbelief keeps the chain on the door and there is no entering while unbelief rules your spirit.

Do any complain that they are required to knock to gain entrance? It is the rule of the Most High God. Am I speaking to any who have been diligent in prayer for months? I can sympathize with you, because I was too, not only for months, but for years. I did not find peace when I first began to ask for it, because my thinking was clouded with cruel, mistaken views of the tenderness of the Lord. My seeking was very serious. I attended church services every time I could and I read the Bible daily with a burning desire to know the right way. I did not enter and find peace until I had knocked long and hard. Therefore, listen to someone who knows your trouble and hear me as I speak with the voice of reason.

Should we really expect to enter the glorious house of mercy without knocking at its door? Do we not expect the same thing with our own homes? Can anyone one just stroll into our house? Does not God's natural world teach us this? The Lord gives great blessings to mankind, but people must knock for them. We need food from the earth, but the farmer must knock at the door of the earth with his plough and all his implements of agriculture before his God will open a harvest to him. Is anything obtained in this world without labor? Is there not truth in that old proverb, "No sweat, no sweet; no pain, no gain; no mill, no meal?" And should we not expect the same principle to apply in heavenly things? Great mercies should be prayed for intensely before they are granted.

It is the usual rule with God to make us pray before he gives us the blessing. How could it be otherwise? How could someone be saved without prayer? A prayer-less soul is a Christ-less soul. Feeling the need for prayer, being in the habit of prayer, and having a spirit of prayer are all parts of salvation. Unless it can be said of a man, "Behold, he is praying" how can there be any kind of hope that he knows his God and has found peace with God? The Prodigal Son did not come home speechless, nor did he enter his father's house in pouting silence. No, as soon as he saw his father, he cried, "Father, I have sinned against heaven." There must be speech with God, because God does not give a silent salvation.

Besides, being forced to knock at mercy's gate brings us a great blessing even while we are waiting for a response. It teaches us that we must persevere in prayer to God if we expect to experience success. It makes a person grow more serious, because their hunger increases while they are waiting. If they obtained the blessing when they first asked for it, it might seem dirt cheap. But when they are forced to plead over and over they gain a better sense of the value of the mercy for which they are seeking. They also see more of their own unworthiness as they stand outside the gate of mercy, ready to faint with fear, and they grow more serious in his praying. At first, they only ask. Now they begin to seek and add the cries and tears of a broken heart to their prayers. The person is being humbled and awakened. The sorrow they experience while waiting outside the gate is good for them now and also in the future because it increases patience. I believe I could not have been able to comfort other seekers in their distress if I had not been kept waiting out in the cold myself. I have always felt grateful for my early distress because of its later results. Many people, whose experiences are recorded in biographies that should be in Christians' libraries, could never have written those books if they had not been kept waiting, hungry and thirsty, and filled with troubles before the Lord appeared to them.

David, that blessed man after God's own heart, seems to be a model for the experience we all have. In Psalm 40, he pictures himself as sinking in the miry bog, going lower and lower until he cried from the depths, until at last the Lord drew him up from the pit of destruction, and set his feet upon a rock, so that he could tell others what the Lord had done for him. Your heart needs enlarging, dear friend. The Lord intends to prepare you to become a more valuable Christian through these trials. The shovel of mental suffering is digging trenches to hold the water of life. Depend on it, if the ships of prayer do not come home quickly, it is because they are more heavily loaded with blessing. When prayer is a long time waiting for the answer, it will be all the sweeter when the answer is received. It is like well ripened fruit that hangs longer on the tree. If you knock with a heavy heart, you will eventually sing with greater joy. Do not be discouraged because you are kept waiting before a closed door.

A Door Implies a Way In

What is the use of a door if it always remains shut? The wall might as well have remained without a break. I have seen certain houses and public buildings with the form and appearance of doors where there were none. The fake doorway was made to improve the look. But there is nothing false in the house of the Lord. HIS DOORS ARE MEANT TO OPEN. They were made on purpose for entering. And the blessed gospel of God is made on purpose for you to enter into life and peace. It would be of no use to knock at a wall, but you are right to knock at a door, because it is designed for opening. You will eventually enter if you continue knocking. The gospel is good news for people. How could it be good news if people could sincerely come to Christ and ask for mercy, and then be denied?

I fear that there is a gospel preached by some that sounds more like bad news than good news to searching souls, because it requires so much feeling and preparation on the sinner's part that the message seems more hopeless than cheerful. But know this, the Lord is willing to save all those who are willing to be saved in his own appointed way. A dear brother put it quite well during our last Monday night prayer meeting: "You, oh God, are perfectly satisfied with the Lord Jesus, and if we are satisfied with him, you are satisfied with us." That is the gospel put into a few words. God is satisfied with Christ, and if you are satisfied with Christ, God is satisfied with you. This is the glad news for every person who is willing to accept the sacrifice the Lord Jesus made and the righteousness he has prepared for all who trust in him.

Dear friend, this gospel would not have been sent unless it was intended to be received by sinners. But someone says, "I am such a great sinner." Just so. You are the very person for whom the news of mercy is intended. A gospel is not needed by perfect people. Sinless people need no pardon. No sacrifice is needed if there is no guilt. No atonement is needed where there is no wrongdoing. Those who are healthy do not need a doctor. The physician is for the sick. This door of hope that God has prepared was intended to be an entrance into life and it was intended to be opened to sinners. If it does not open to sinners it will never open at all, because we have all sinned, and we must all be shut out unless it is opened by free grace for those who are guilty.

I am sure this door must open to those who have nothing to bring with them. If you have no good works, no goodness, no good feelings, nothing to recommend you, do not be discouraged. It is to you that Jesus Christ is most precious and therefore most approachable. He loves to give himself to those who prize him the most. A person will never accept Christ while they are satisfied with themself. But the one who is aware that they are naked, poor, and miserable is the person for Christ, because they are the one who has been redeemed at such a great price. You may recognize the person who has been redeemed, because they feel their slavery to sin, and admit that they must remain in it unless the price Christ paid is applied for their release.

Dear friends, that door of hope will be opened to you even though you may be ignorant, and weak, and quite unable to fulfill any high expectations. When the Bible says, "Knock, and it will be opened to you," it teaches us that the way of gaining admission to the blessing is simple and appropriate for common people. If I need to enter in by a door that is well secured, I will need tools and knowledge. I do not understand the art. You must send for a gentleman who understands lock picks, jimmies, and all kinds of burglary tools. But if I am only told to knock, fool as I am at opening doors, I know how to knock. Any uneducated person can knock if that is all that is required of them. Is there a person here who cannot put words together to say a prayer? Never mind, friend. Knocking can be done by one who is not a skilled public speaker. Perhaps someone else complains, "I am no scholar." Never mind, a someone who is not well educated can still knock. A mute person can knock. A blind person can knock. A disabled person may knock. Someone who knows nothing at all can still lift a door knocker and let it fall. The way to open heaven's gate is wonderfully simple. Those who are lowly enough to follow the Holy Spirit's guidance only need to believe and ask, believe and seek, and believe and knock. God has not provided a salvation that can only be understood by highly educated people. He has not prepared a gospel that requires half-a-dozen large books to describe it. It is for the uneducated, the short-witted, and the dying, as well as for others. Therefore it must be as plain as knocking at a door. This is it. Believe and live. Seek for God with all your heart and soul, and strength, through Jesus Christ, and the door of his mercy will certainly open to you. The gate of grace is meant to give admission to uneducated people since it will be opened to those who knock.

I am sure this door will open to you, because it has been opened to so many before you. It has been opened to hundreds of us who are here now. Dear brothers and sisters, if I asked you now, could you not stand up and tell us how the Lord opened the gate of his salvation to you? That door has opened to many in this building during the last few weeks. We have seen people coming forward to tell how the Lord has been pleased to give them entrance into his mercy, even though at one time they were afraid that the door was shut against them, and they were ready to lose hope. Well, if the door has been opened so often for others, why should its hinges not turn for you? Just knock, with faith in God's mercy, and before long it will give way to your persistence.

God is glorified when he opens his door of grace and that is one reason why we are sure he will do it. We cannot expect him to do what would dishonor him, but we do expect him to do what will glorify his holy character. It will greatly honor the mercy, the patience, the love, the grace, the goodness, and the favor of God if he will open the door to someone as undeserving as you are. Therefore knock! Knock because God delights to give. Knock at a door that reveals God's greatness every time it turns on its hinges. Knock with holy confidence at this very moment, because "it will be opened to you." It is a door that seems closed, but because it is a door it must be capable of being opened.

A Door Knocker Is Provided

When people can be let in by knocking, a door knocker is usually placed on the door. Otherwise, we often see the words NO ADMITTANCE. Before doorbells became so common the habit of knocking at the door was almost universal and people were accustomed to make the door boom with their blows. There was a strike plate (or nailhead) for the knocker to drop on. People used to strike it so heavily that some said the blows were killing. That is where the amusing proverb, "As dead as a door nail" came from. It indicates a wholehearted kind of knocking, the kind I would have you imitate in prayer. Knock at heaven's gate as intensely as people knocked at doors in the olden days. Have you not had knocks at your own doors that could be heard throughout the house? Some of our friends are vigorous and knock as if they meant to come in. It may be that gentle folks give such tender taps that no one in the house can hear them, and so they have to wait. But the ones I am talking about never fall into that error, because they startle everyone so much that people are glad to let them in, for fear they should thunder a second time. Pray that way. Let us plead downright earnestly and never stop until we gain entrance.

I have said THE LORD HAS PROVIDED A DOOR KNOCKER. What is this door knocker? First of all, it is found in the promises of God. We are sure to succeed when we can appeal to a promise. It is good to say to the Lord, "Do as you have said." There is great force in a prayer that appeals to the word, the promise, and the covenant of God. If someone presents a promissory note on the day that it is due, he expects to receive the amount indicated. God's promises are promissory notes and he will honor them. He has never dishonored a promise yet and he never will. If you can just quote a promise that applies to your situation, and spread it before the Lord in faith, and say, "Remember this promise to your servant on which you have caused me to hope," you must obtain the blessing. Pleading the promise gives such a knock at the gate of heaven that it must be opened.

The great door knocker, however, is the name of the Lord Jesus Christ. If a person were to call on you in the name of some dearly loved son who is far away, if he brought you proper documentation and a letter, saying, "Father treat this person well for my sake," you would be sure to show him kindness. And if this person were authorized to receive a promised amount of money in the name of your son, would you not give it to him? Now, when we go to God and plead the name of Christ, it means that we plead the authority of Christ, that we ask from God as though we were in Christ's place, and expect him to give it to us as if he were giving it to Jesus. This is more than pleading for Christ's sake. I suppose the apostles at first pleaded with God for Christ's sake, but Jesus said to them, "Until now you have asked nothing *in my name.*" It is a higher level of prayer. When we pray to the Father in Christ's name we wonderfully succeed.

At a Primitive Methodist meeting someone was trying to pray, but could not get the words out. And then a voice was heard from the corner of the room, "Plead the blood, brother! Plead the blood!" I am not very fond of such interruptions, but this was commendable, because it gave sound advice and put the person praying on solid ground. Plead the precious blood of Jesus Christ and you have knocked in a way that must be heard.

Someone says, "Alas! I see the door knocker, that is, I know something about the promises and of the person of our Lord, but how am I to knock?" Knock with the hand of faith. Believe that God will keep his promise. Ask him to do so and knock accordingly. You are praying in Jesus' name. Believe that he is worthy and knock with the confidence that God will honor the name of his dear Son. "My hand is too weak," you say. Then remember that the Holy Spirit helps us in our weakness. Ask him to place his hand on your hand, and in that way you will be able to knock with the strength needed to succeed. I plead with you to knock with all the strength you have and to knock often.

My dear hearer, if you are not in Christ, do not give sleep to your eyes nor slumber to your eyelids until you have found the Lord Jesus. If you have prayed once, go and pray again. And if you have prayed ten thousand times, yet continue in prayer. Knock with all your might, with all the strength of your spirit. Plead as if pleading for your life. Knock at the door as someone would knock who saw a wolf ready to attack him. Knock as someone would knock who found himself ready to die of cold outside the door. Throw your whole soul into the work. Say to the Lord, " I appeal to you to have mercy on me and to have mercy on me now. I faint, I die, unless you show your love to me and take me into your house and heart, so that I may be yours forever." "Knock, and it will be opened to you." There is the door knocker.

A Promise Is Given to Those Who Knock

Next, A PROMISE IS GIVEN TO THOSE KNOCKING AT THE GATE. This is more than having a door in front of you or a door knocker to knock with. The promise is written above the gate in plain words. Read it. You are growing tired and faint. Read the promise and grow strong again. "Knock, and it will be opened to you." Notice how plain and positive it is with its glorious "will" burning like a lamp in the center of it. Each letter is written in love and the message shines out in the darkness that surrounds you, and these are its words, "It will be opened to you." If you knock at the door of the kindest of men, there is no promise like this over their door, but you still knock and you knock with confidence. How much more boldly should you come to the door of grace when it is clearly declared, "It will be opened to you!"

Remember that his promise was freely given. You never asked the Lord for such a promise, it was the result of his natural goodness. You did not come and plead with Jesus for a promise that you would be heard in prayer. Far from it—you did not even pray. Perhaps you have been living in the world forty years and have never truly prayed at all. But out of his overflowing heart of generous love the Lord made this promise to you, "Knock, and it will be opened to you." Why do you doubt? Do you think he will not keep his word? A God who cannot lie, who was under no obligation to make a promise, freely, out of the greatness of his divine nature, which is love, says to a poor sinner, "Knock, and it will be opened to you." Oh, be sure of this; he means it! Jesus said, "Heaven and earth will pass away, but my words will not pass away." Neither you nor any other sinner who knocks at his door will be refused.

These words have encouraged many to knock. When they have been ready to faint and give up seeking anymore, they have read the cheering lines again, "Knock, and it will be opened to you," and they have taken heart and made the door thunder again. Now, do you think God will tease us, that he will make fools of us, that he will stir up hope in poor sinners, just so that he can disappoint them? Will he encourage you to knock by his promise and then laugh at you? Did the God of mercy ever say, "I called and you came; I stretched out my hands and you drew near to me, and yet I will mock at your affliction, and laugh when your fear comes"? Why, even a bad man would hardly talk like that. It would be more like Satan than God to act that way. Do not accept the thought that the God of all grace would treat a seeker like that. If it ever crosses your mind, shove it away and say, "He who taught me to pray has obligated himself to answer my prayer. He will not invite me to knock in vain! Therefore, I will knock again, only this time harder than ever, and I will rely on his word and his truth." Oh, that you will never stop knocking until you have gained entrance through salvation's door. The promise of the Lord was given freely and we knock on the strength of that promise. Therefore, we are sure that the Lord will not refuse his trusting servants.

The great blessing is that this promise is meant for any and all who knock. "Knock, and it will be opened to you." The Lord has not denied to you the privilege of praying nor has he declared that he will not answer your requests. You may knock and you may fully expect to see the door open. I know the blessed doctrine of election and I rejoice in it; but that is a secret with God, while the rule of our preaching is, "Proclaim the gospel to the whole creation." Therefore, I say to each person here, "Knock, and it will be opened to you." The Lord knows who will knock, because, "the Lord knows those who are his."

My friend, knock, and knock now, and it will soon be seen that you are one of God's chosen ones. Do you remember the story of Malachi from Cornwall? When a Methodist friend had some money to give him he smiled and said, "Malachi, I do not think I will give you this money, because I do not know whether you are predestinated to have it. Can you tell me whether you are predestinated to have it or not?" Malachi replied, "Put the money in my hand and I will tell you." As soon as Malachi had the money in hand he knew that he was predestinated to have it; but he could not know he had it until it was in his possession. The secret counsel of the Lord is revealed to our faith when it possesses Christ and not before. Knock immediately. If you are predestinated to enter, I know you will knock, and you will knock until the door is opened to you. That is the promise and no exception is made to it. "Knock, and it will be opened to you." It is a rule with the Lord that to everyone who knocks it will be opened.

Bless God. This text of mine shines out as if printed in stars and it continues to shine from the dawning of the day of life to the setting of the sun in death. As long as a person lives, if they knock at God's door, it will be opened to them. You may have rebelled against God for a long time, and you may have piled up your sins until they seem to shut out all hope for you, but still, knock at Christ the door, because a time of opening will come. Even if you were about to breathe your last, if you could knock at mercy's gate it would open for you. But do not put off your day of knocking because of God's patient mercy. Knock today, knock now while sitting in the pew and if you are not answered immediately, as I trust you will be, yet go home, and there in secret cry to the Lord, "I will not let you go unless you bless me. I am lost unless you find me. I am lost unless I find my Savior and Lord. I am not playing at prayer now, my very soul means it. I must have Christ or else I die just as I am. I cast myself on him and trust his atoning sacrifice. Oh reveal yourself to me as a pardoning God!" I am living proof that God will answer you. I sought the Lord and he heard me. And since then I have never doubted that any living soul that seeks the Lord through Jesus Christ will certainly be saved. Oh, that you would try it! May the Lord move in you to do so by his own blessed Spirit.

It Will Be a Glorious Opening for You

So I close with one more point. When the door opens IT WILL BE A GLORIOUS OPENING FOR YOU. "Knock, and it will be opened."

What will happen? As soon as you have knocked you will enter. If you have knocked in sincerity, the moment you see Christ as a Savior you will accept him as your Savior. Enter into Christ by faith. See, he sets an open door before you and no one can shut it. Do not hesitate to enter in. Up to this point you have thought there were many difficulties and obstacles in your way, but really there were not. Believe and live! When, in answer to your knocking, you see the door move, then enter in, and do not wait.

Remember that the opening of that door will not only give you entrance, but it will guarantee your safety. Once someone enters into Christ he is safe forever. Once you pass through that blood-sprinkled doorway, once you have entered into the joy of the Well-Beloved Master, you will be safe inside forever. The life that he gives is eternal; therefore, you will not die. The destroying angel, whenever he may take his flight, must pass you by. Only believe and you are saved. Only trust Christ with your whole heart, and soul, and strength and salvation has come to your house, and you have come to the house of salvation.

This house will be yours because you will have been adopted into God's family. Once you enter you will live in the palace of grace, no more a stranger or a guest, but you will be like a child at home. You will sit at the Father's table and eat and drink as a son or daughter, an heir, a joint-heir with Christ. You will have the liberty, the plenty, and the joy of the great house of love. There are pleasures for evermore at God's right hand and they will be your inheritance. Yes, and more than that. When you have once entered into the house of love you will have access to its inner rooms. Even the entryway of God's house is a place of safety, but afterwards the Master of the house will take you into wonderful rooms, and show you his treasures, and open his storehouses to you, so that you will go from grace to grace, from knowledge to knowledge, and glory to glory, as you continually progress. All of this can only be understood by experience and that experience can only be gained by knocking.

I want to say this and then I am finished. Some people think if they have begun to pray and are a little serious that this is enough. Now, praying is not an end, it is only a means. Knocking is not the final step. You must enter in. If any of you are seeking, I am glad that you are; if you are knocking, I am glad that you are; but if you say, "I am perfectly satisfied to stand outside the door and knock," then I am grieved for you. You are foolish to the nth degree, because you are depending on the means as if it were the end. You must enter by the door or else knocking will be labor in vain.

Would any of you be content to visit a friend and merely stand for an hour or two outside of his door knocking? Did you ever say, "I do not need anything more. I will sit down comfortably on the doorstep and then get up every once in a while and have another knock or two"? Knocking would not get you a dinner, nor do your business for you. Knocking is only the way of entrance, but if all you do is knock, it is poor work. The most earnest praying is only a way of getting to Christ. The gospel is, "Believe in the Lord Jesus, and you will be saved." Come to Christ. If you find the door shut, knock. But oh, remember, the door is not really shut. It only seems to be. Heaven's gate stands open night and day. As soon as you believe you live. Trust in the work of Jesus Christ and you are clothed in his righteousness. Trust in the blood of Christ and you are washed in it. Faith saves in an instant. Faith touches Jesus and the healing power pours out from him. Faith steps over the threshold and the soul is safe.

May the Lord grant that you may enter in at once, and then it will be our joy, and the angels' joy, and the great Father's joy, forever and ever, to see you rescued from destruction!

FREE PARDON

A Sermon Delivered
by C. H. Spurgeon at the Metropolitan Tabernacle, London
Scripture read before sermon: Isaiah 43:22-28 & Isaiah 44:1-22

Isaiah 43:25

"I, I am he who blots out your transgressions for my own sake, and I will not remember your sins."

Introduction

This extraordinary passage becomes all the more remarkable when considered in its context. It follows a description of the sins of God's people; a description that includes their sins of omission as well as commission. They had neglected the service of the Most High. The Lord says, "You have not brought me your sheep for burnt offerings or honored me with your sacrifices." Their sins of commission had gone so far in breaking God's law that they had even wearied him with their iniquities. The charges against God's people are clear. A thousand facts prove it. Nothing can be said to make them seem less serious than they are. We might expect the next words from the divine Judge to be the order for their execution. But, wonder of wonders, there comes a full canceling of the charges, a complete pardon! "I, I am he who blots out your transgressions." (Oh Jehovah, who is a pardoning God like you?)

This verse is followed by more verses that continue to convict the people of great sins. The Lord asks them to come and plead their case with him, if they think they can. He gives them an opportunity to speak for themselves, if they have anything to say by way of excusing their faults. Then he tells them they had sinned as a nation from the very beginning and still continue to sin. The Lord knew he would add more words to show his disapproval, but before he concluded his charge against them, he paused in the very middle of his righteous accusation, to tell them he had already forgiven them. He said, "I, I am he who blots out your transgressions for my own sake." The remarkable point is not merely that the pardon is found preceded and succeeded by verses of accusation, but that it breaks the connection and splits the sense right down the middle.

The king's messenger of mercy rides through the ranks of the soldiers in great haste, sounding his silver bugle as he clears his way. He cannot stop. His message is too precious to allow him to linger. The sun and moon may stand still sooner than mercy may be delayed. Breaks in the text like this are very precious to me, because they show the intense love of God for his works of grace and his eagerness to perform them. I love these soft showers of grace and mercy even more because they break in so unexpectedly on the tremendous peals of the thunder of well-deserved wrath.

We will be wise to not only consider the text, but to notice the practical lesson it contains. Since God is certain to reveal his mercy when it will be most valued, we may conclude that people will be aware and prize divine mercy most when they feel the weight of their sins the most. A man will not ask for mercy until he is aware of his condemnation and pleads guilty. If he did not think he was guilty, he would sneer at mercy if he were offered it. He would be insulted by the offer of forgiveness. What else would a pardon offered to an innocent person be except an insult? We might as well send medicine to someone who was never sick or give a handout to a millionaire!

We must be proven guilty and confess it before we can be forgiven. We must know that we are sick and we must clearly recognize that our sickness is a terminal disease or else we will never value the divine medicine that Jesus came to bring. A sense of sin is exceedingly painful, but it is a great blessing. If you have never felt how guilty you are, I pray to God that you may be made to feel it now. If you have never been humbled before the awful majesty of divine justice, may the Holy Spirit break you down now. Jesus will never clothe those who are not stripped of their polluted garments. He will never wash those who are not dirty, nor will he attempt to heal those who are not wounded. Others may spend their strength in flattering human goodness, but the Lord Jesus has come on another errand. He deals only with our sin and misery. If you are not poverty stricken, you will have no dealings with the blessed soul enriching Savior.

Now that we have considered the verse in its context, let us notice two other points. The first is the kind of the pardon that is so graciously proclaimed here. The second is the effect that this pardon produces on the minds of those who are given the means to receive it.

The Kind of Pardon Declared

My dear friends, let us carefully consider THE KIND OF PARDON THAT IS SO GRACIOUSLY ANNOUNCED here. "I, I am he who blots out your transgressions for my own sake, and I will not remember your sins." First, notice it is a pardon from God himself. Second, observe that it is a pardon from the God who has been offended. Sin is mainly an attack on God. It is an offense against his own most excellent person. It is treason against his most glorious sovereignty. Therefore, God feels more, sees more and is more thoroughly affected by the evil of sin than anyone else. The context shows that he does not treat sin as unimportant, like some do. He does not regard it as something that can be easily passed over. He takes serious note of the sinful omissions and commissions of his people. In due time he calls them to account, mentioning their sins in a way that shows he is greatly displeased. In Jehovah's eyes, sin is extremely bad. It is horrible and hated. Yet, it is the very same God who has such a hatred of sin who says, "I, I am he who blots out your transgressions." We have offended God and the same offended God forgives us. We have violated his law and yet the lawgiver himself pardons us. We have insulted his majesty and yet the King himself comes down from his throne and says, "I, I am he who blots out your transgressions."

This is even more wonderful because we know that only he could forgive us. What is the use of forgiveness from one who has not been offended? How can I forgive you for a crime that you have committed against someone else? The power to forgive lives only in the great Supreme Being. If you receive pardon from him, it is a pardon beyond all question. If some man, like yourself, claims that he has received a commission from heaven to acquit you, it is not worth the breath he spends in uttering the fake absolution, or the time you waste listening to it. But if the Lord himself, out of his excellent glory, says, "I, I am he who blots out your transgressions," then the pardon is certainly divine and effective.

There is substance in divine forgiveness, it is not a dream or figment of the imagination. Who can condemn the person whom God forgives? This led the apostle Paul to say, "Who shall bring any charge against God's elect? It is God who justifies. Who is to condemn?" The Lord's forgiveness brings deep peace to the soul. If he has said, "I forgive you" to the greatest offender, what more is needed? What is the use of adding ceremonies and rituals, and the like, if the Lord, himself, has spoken? One word from the lips of Jehovah, the great forgiving God, is worth millions of masses, and billions of indulgences from the Pope himself. Our conscience seeks nothing more than pardon from the Lord and it will never be satisfied with anything less. Oh Lord, it is you we have wronged and your own sure word of grace satisfies us. Without your Spirit speaking that word, our heart continues to condemn us and we waste away in our sins.

Brothers and sisters, there is something about the character of God that is not always talked about as much as it should be. It is something that tends to make his forgiveness even more comforting to the soul. There are many idolaters in the world besides those who worship blocks of wood and stone. There are people who would look down on anyone who called them idolaters, but they are! Rather than worshiping the true God, they, too, have a god of their own making. They have not made him with wood, or clay, or gold, or silver, but they have constructed him from their own perceptions. They believe in a god like they think God ought to be. He is made to fit the fashion of the times. The god they invent for themselves is a being entirely without justice. They say that the God of the Bible (who is the real, living and true God who made the heavens and the earth) is vindictive, because he punishes rebellion against his law severely, because, being in charge of an entirely moral government, he will not permit his law to be trampled on without punishment, and will not clear the guilty. The God who punishes sinners and does not accept less than perfect works is not the God for modern people. They want an easier deity, a less strict god. They want a god who is only as virtuous as they are. The Lord God of Elijah will never suit the soft spoken Ahabs of this age who cry, "Peace, peace," where there is no peace. The God of the Bible has never been loved by the proud and worldly.

The world wants a god of their own making, who is like themselves, who cares nothing about the evil of sin and will wink at it, and will allow sinners to go unpunished. They want a god who does their bidding, who quenches the fires of hell, or at least limits its punishment to a few years. Theirs is a god who gives them license to think as they like and treat his word as so much clay to mold and fashion to their own desires. The god of modern thought is not the God of the Bible. He is no more the true God than Baal or Ashtaroth, Jupiter or Apollo.

The true God is the God who is revealed in the Scriptures and made known in the person of the Lord Jesus Christ. He is known only to those to whom he reveals himself. The rest, by their own worldly wisdom, are blinded so that they have not seen him or known him. If there were a god whose nature was nothing except gentleness and who winked at sin, his pardon would never satisfy my conscience. When my conscience was awakened to know the evil of sin, I felt that if God did not punish me, he ought to. My heart felt that my sin should not go unpunished. In fact, I punished myself for my sin by the deep convictions, fears and trembling of my soul. If anyone had said

God blots out sin and thinks no more about it, their assurance would have given me no peace. I would have felt that my pardon involved an injustice. My sin would still have cried for vengeance and therefore my conscience would have had no peace.

When I came to understand that the God of the Bible would not pardon sin without first upholding the honor of his moral government, that he would not allow sin to be trifled with and go unpunished and that, therefore he, himself, in the person of his own Son had suffered the penalty for my sin; then I said, "This is the kind of pardon I need. A pardon that satisfies God's justice and therefore satisfies my own instincts of right and wrong. The Lord Jesus, bearing my sins in his own body on the cross, makes me feel perfectly content, because now God, himself, cannot bring any charge against me, because he cannot punish me for what he has already laid on his own Son." Will he demand payment twice for one debt or punish one offense twice?

If my sins were laid on his Son, then God's justice is more than satisfied and my soul accepts the free pardon he gives. There is no fear that the strictest justice will ever declare my pardon invalid. When Jehovah, the God of the Bible, says, "I, I am he who blots out your transgressions, I am he who thundered from the top of Mt. Sinai, who drowned Pharaoh and his army in the Red Sea, I am he who struck down Sennacherib and all his warriors, I, the just and terrible God, who revenges and is furious, and whose anger burns like fire against sin, I, even I, am he who blots out your transgressions," these are glorious words indeed. The Lord is "a righteous God and a Savior." He is both "just and the justifier of the one who has faith in Jesus." Here is a solid foundation for the heart. Here is rest for the conscience. This is pardon that changes the scales to our favor. This is pardon that relieves the wounds of conscience and breathes life into hearts dying of despair.

So, you see, there is a great deal in the fact that the pardon comes from God. But I have not finished. Remember beloved, that since pardon comes from God, and since he, and he alone, knows how great our sin really is, he is also fully aware how great his pardon really is. A man being might pardon an offense against himself, but not know the full extent of the offense. He might soon wake up to a fuller sense of the offense committed against him and feel new anger at the offender. A king can only forgive a rebel for the acts of which he knows he is guilty. The Lord knows all our sins. There is not a sin that has ever escaped his eyes. He knows those committed in secret, in the darkness of the night. He knows those that never struggled into action, sins of the heart and imagination that are known only to you and God. What does he not see? This is a blessing for us, because it means our pardon covers the full extent of our sin.

A priest once said that if we did not remember all our sins, and confess them, they would never be forgiven. If that is true, then certainly no one will be forgiven, because no one can ever remember one-thousandth of their sins. But praise God, the pardon does not depend on our knowledge of the sin, but with God's knowledge of the sin. Therefore, the pardon that comes from the all-seeing God is complete. "I, I am he," the all-powerful and ever-present God, who saw you in the darkness and heard your heart in all its evil speeches against the Most High, I, the all-knowing one, "I am he who blots out your transgressions."

This is unrivaled pardon that brings complete comfort. Every aspect of God adds to its richness. Every beam of divine glory reveals more splendor. When we realize it is our Father, our heavenly Father whom we have offended, who now kisses us with the kisses of love and hugs us close, and says, "I, I am he who blots out your transgressions," the pardon becomes infinitely more precious.

The Reason the Pardon is Given

Why is this pardon given? On what basis is it granted? THE REASON IS EXTREMELY COMFORTING. "For my own sake." The entire motive of God for forgiving sin lies within himself. "For my own sake." No one has their sins forgiven because they are little, because the smallest sin will ruin the soul. Every sin is great, however small it may seem to us. Each sin has the essence of rebellion in it and rebellion is a great evil before God. Therefore, no one will have God say to them, "I have blotted out your sins because they were so small." Never.

No one's sin is forgiven because their repentance is praiseworthy. There is nothing in Scripture to suggest such an idea. Repentance comes before a sense of forgiveness in some degree, but it comes more after forgiveness. Repentance is not the cause of forgiveness, even though it is seen with forgiveness. God's motive for pardoning a sinner is not because that sinner repents. God does not demand repentance as some kind of payment before he will forgive. The lost in hell feel a repentance (I think I had better call it *remorse*), but it does not change their doom. If not for a Savior, we might have had repentance like Esau felt when he "lifted up his voice and wept," but his repentance did not keep him from losing the blessing. He lost it forever.

Neither does our text tell us that God forgives people's sins because he believes they will do better after they are forgiven. God's grace makes people better, but it is not foreseeing any improvement on their part that leads God to forgive them. That cannot be God's motive, because if they do better, their improvement is his work in them. Left to themselves they would do even worse after they were pardoned than they had done before. They would argue God's mercy gives them a license to sin. Sadly, too many have already done so. No. The only motive that God has for pardoning sinners, according to the text, is one that lies with himself: "For my own sake."

And what is that motive? Brothers and sisters, the Lord knows his motives and it is not for us to judge them. But, first, is it not so he can take pleasure in his mercy? Of all God's attributes, he uses mercy last, but it is the one that pleases him most. The Lord blots out sin, because he is full of mercy. Another motive is to glorify his Son, who is one with the Father. His Son has made atonement. He has offered and presented it. And now, so that he may have his full reward, the Lord delights to blot out the sins of those who come to him. The motive lies in God himself. What a comfort this is. If I look into my soul, I cannot see any reason why God should save me. But I do not need to be concerned, because the motive lies in our gracious God alone.

The reason he blots out my transgressions is because of his great loving kindness. I may look to all my past life and not discover a solitary action that I could point to in making a plea for mercy. I may look to my present condition and not detect even a glimpse of improvement, or even a ray of hope that I will be better in the future. In fact, I will only have the dreadful fear that I will grow worse and worse. When I have seen these discouraging facts, I have only seen what is the truth, I have only seen how unworthy my case is. But there is comfort for me. I may look away from myself to God. It is my duty to do so. Oh friend, if God is to save you, it will not be because of anything you are or will ever be. He must save you for his own sake.

The door of mercy is open! It is not open only a little, so only those who are little sinners may enter. The great gate of grace stands wide open. What if I say it is nailed back to the wall? What sinner is there whom God cannot pardon, if he pardons for his own sake and not for the sinner's sake? What if someone were black with lusts that we dare not mention? What if he were red with murder? What if he had committed every crime in the catalog of guilt If God pardons, not because of anything he sees in the person, but because of what he finds in himself, it remains a possibility for God to pardon the vilest of the vile. The truth revealed in the Bible makes it certain that God will forgive even the worst if they turn to him, confess their sins, believe in his dear Son, and so pass from death to life. How wonderful it is to look not only at the God who gives the pardon, but also at the reason why he gives it. "For my own sake."

The Pardon is Complete and Thorough

This glorious text is important because it declares HOW COMPLETE AND THOROUGH THE PARDON IS. The Lord does not say, "I, I am he that blots out *some* of your transgressions and will not remember *a certain number* of your sins." No, the Lord makes a clean sweep of the whole dreadful heap of our sins. They are all driven away instantly by one stroke of almighty mercy. The text includes all the sins the Lord had mentioned before. "You have not bought me sweet cane with money or satisfied me with the fat of your sacrifices." They would not pay for the ingredients for the incense used in the temple or sacrifice any more animals than absolutely required by the law. Our *sins of omission* are all gone. Beloved friends, can any of us count our sins of omission? They are the sins that ruin people. At the last great day the Judge will say "to those on his left," "I was hungry and you gave me no food, I was thirsty and you gave me no drink, I was a stranger and you did not welcome me, naked and you did not clothe me, sick and in prison and you did not visit me." They were not condemned for what they did do, but for what they did not do. The majority of our sins are the things we have not done, the things we have left undone which should have been done. Who can count them? They outnumber the sands of the ocean. Yet the divine pardon cleanses us from them all. No spot or wrinkle remains.

And then he mentions *actual sins.* He says, "You have burdened me with your sins." But then he declares that he blots them out, sins of omission and commission, both forms of evil. They are both gone, all gone, entirely gone.

I do not know what particular sins the members of this congregation may have committed. Suppose we were to begin at that aisle over there, and each one had to stand up and confess his sins? Well, it would take a great amount of time and we would have sinned a great deal more before we had come to the end of the confession. What a pile of sin there would be on this threshing floor if every person were compelled to bring his own mass of sin and pour it out on the common heap. But the Lord does not set limits. He says, "I, I am he who blots out your transgressions and I will not remember your sins." All the believer's sins are gone and they are all gone immediately.

This is the joy and glory of gospel forgiveness. The believer knows that his sins are not in the process of being pardoned, but are actually pardoned at this moment. No shred of our sins remains to be dealt with in the future, the whole pile is swept away. However black the guilt, however serious the offense, however repeated the crime, however wicked because committed against light, however enormous because committed with contempt for the Holy Spirit, they are annihilated. When we believe in Jesus Christ, they are gone forever. Sins against God's law and word and day, sins against Christ's blood, sins against his love, sins against his person, sins against Christ in all his offices, an infinite variety of sins vanish before that gracious declaration, "I, I am he who blots out your transgressions."

The pardon is remarkable because it is completely effective. It is described as blotting out. Blotting out is a very thorough way of deciding something. If a debt on a ledger has been outstanding for a long time and the pen is drawn through it, it remains no longer. Whether it is a large amount or a small one, the same stroke of the pen will do it. If you owed a creditor $50,000.00 and someone else owed him only $1,000.00, the word PAID takes as many strokes of the pen to write for one account as the other. And if the creditor is satisfied, it is just as easily done for one as the other. Whatever sin there may have been in God's people when they come before him, he writes ACQUITTED at the bottom of the page. Its power to condemn is gone. What a joy it is to see the long list of my sins blotted out by the bleeding hands of Jesus, so that it cannot be read in the court of heavenly justice. What great happiness to see it nailed to the cross of the dying Savior. As heavy as my soul's debts were, I doubt no longer, because I see the grim punishment nailed to the bloody tree.

Notice that wonderful expression, "I will not remember your sins." Can God forget? Forgetting with God cannot be an impairment like it is with us. We forget because our memory fails, but God forgets in the blessed sense that he remembers the merit of his Son rather than our sins. God forgets sin in the sense that he remembers it is forgiven. I think it was Augustine (who had once been a great sinner) who after he was converted was met in the street by one with whom he had often fallen into sin. When she spoke to him and said, "Augustine, it is I," he said, "Ah, but it is not *I*, I am dead, and made alive again." When God's justice meets a person who believes in Jesus, that person is no longer the *I* that sinned, because that *I* is dead in Christ.

"We know that our old self was crucified with him." The believer was buried with Christ and those who are dead are free from the law that condemned them. How can the law arrest a dead person? So, we who are dead in Christ and risen again in him are new creatures, and do not come under the divine sentence. God now knows us not as sinners, but as new creatures in Christ Jesus. He knows and recognizes in us the new life, because "he has caused us to be born again to a living hope through the resurrection of Jesus Christ from the dead." That is one of the instructive features of baptism. In baptism the believer pictures the doctrine of salvation by death and burial. That was Noah's salvation. He went into the ark as one dead to the world. He was buried in the ark and then he floated out from the old world into the new. The apostle Peter mentioned Noah and the ark and said, "Baptism, which corresponds to this, now saves you, not as a removal of dirt from the body but as an appeal to God for a good conscience, through the resurrection of Jesus Christ." That is, baptism is a picture of salvation, because it illustrates our death with Christ, our burial with Christ, and our resurrection with Christ.

Where there is true faith and the soul has fellowship with Christ, we are dead and buried with him in baptism, "in order that, just as Christ was raised from the dead by the glory of the Father, we too might walk in newness of life." Death has come upon us, "because we have concluded this," says the apostle Paul, "that one has died for all, therefore all have died; and he died for all, that those who live might no longer live for themselves but for him who for their sake died and was raised." Beloved, in that case, if we are dead, then I am not surprised that God says he does not remember our sins, because we are new creatures and we have passed from death to life. We have come into a new life and God looks on us from a new point of view. He sees us from a new perspective; not as offspring of the first Adam condemned and dead, but of the second Adam, the Lord from heaven, the living and life giving Spirit. He is justified in saying to people who are new creatures, "I will not remember your sins."

Every word of our text is delightful. I cannot take time to go into the fullness of it. May the Lord lead each of you to explore it more fully, especially you young people. And may those who are not converted desire the precious things it talks about. May God speak to some who came in here shameful sinners and say to them, "For my own sake I forgive you." You will leap for joy! What a thrill will go through your heart! I guarantee you will no longer doubt the existence of God. You will have no more questions and objections. The Spirit of God will speak to your heart and that will convince you though nothing else will. You will leave this place to glorify the grace you once despised.

The Effect of This Pardon

I now come to the consideration of THE EFFECT OF THIS PARDON wherever it comes with power to the soul.

Some are fearful that the free pardon of sin will lead people to indulge in it. And some, no doubt, are wicked enough to pervert pardon in that way.

But there was never a soul that really did receive pardon from God who could find any excuse for sin in that pardon or any license to continue in sin any longer. All God's people argue this way: "Are we to continue in sin that grace may abound? By no means! How can we who died to sin still live in it?" The apostle Paul also said, "Are we to sin because we are not under law but under grace? By no means!" These are serious disclaimers against the idea that the amazing mercy of God can lead the regenerate into sin.

The first effect of pardon on the person who receives it is surprise. This person has been sitting at the foot of the cross looking for mercy when all of a sudden he glances at the bleeding Savior and is forgiven. He feels something like Peter when the angel brought him out of the prison. "He did not know that what was being done by the angel was real, but thought he was seeing a vision."

> When God revealed his gracious name,
>   And changed our mournful state,
> Our rapture seemed a pleasing dream;
>   The grace appeared too great.

I remember how overjoyed I was when I received pardon. I was surprised and staggered by the thought. I was so delighted I did not know how to contain myself. But after a while I was plagued by this thought: "Such great mercy is too good to be true." How could it be that I was actually forgiven? How could it be that I had been made clean in the sight of God through the blood of Jesus? The goodness of God astounded me.

It reminds me of an illustration I have used before, but it is a good one. If you have a dog at the table and throw him a scrap of meat, he swallows it in one gulp. But if you were to set the whole steak down on the floor, he would turn away. He would feel that you could not mean to give a fine steak to a dog. He would not think of touching it—at least, most would not. It seemed to me as if the Lord could not have meant all the wonders of his love to be given to such a dog as I was. I was ready to turn away from it because it was so great. But then I remembered that it would not do for a great God to be giving little mercy. He was too great to spend all his power in pardoning little sinners and granting little favors. I came back to this: If his grace was not too big for him to give, I should not be such a fool as to refuse it because of its greatness.

Alexander the Great once told a soldier that he could have whatever he asked. The man went to the royal treasury and demanded such a huge amount that the officer refused to let him have it. He said to the soldier,

"How can you be such an unreasonable person and ask for so much? When Alexander heard of it he said, "It is much for him to receive, but it is not too much for Alexander to give. He has a high opinion of my greatness. Let him have what he has asked for. I will not fall short of his expectations." God is a great God and to forgive great sins is just like him. We cannot forgive like this, but God can. To forgive great sins, tremendous sins, unspeakably black sins, adds to his glory and makes people say, "Who is a God like you, pardoning iniquity and passing over transgression?"

Mercy fills us with surprise. The next thing it does is fill us with holy regret. We feel, "What? Is this the God I have been opposing for so long? Is this the God I have despised or neglected, whose gospel I have rejected, saying that there was time enough for me to look into it when I grew old and had seen a little of life? Is this the God I have been slighting, who has loved me so greatly, and given his dear Son from his own right hand to bleed and suffer in my place?"

I think it was Aristotle who said that a person cannot know that he is loved without feeling some degree of love in return. I am quite certain that you cannot know in your soul, by the experience of pardon, that God loves you, without immediately feeling, "I am ashamed that I did not love my gracious God. I am disgusted with myself that I could have acted in such a disgraceful way toward him. Did he love me before the world began? Did he write my name in the book of his electing love? Did he decree that I should wear a crown of life and have a harp of gold? Did he predestine me to be conformed to the image of his Son? When the Savior bled, did he think of me as he was dying? Did he lay down his life especially for me? Am I one whom he has pledged to himself forever in faithfulness and love and mercy? Have I been foolish enough to live all this time a stranger and enemy to him?" When a sense of such dying love comes rushing into our heart, we feel like taking revenge on our cruel hearts for treating such a generous and such a forgiving God the way we did.

This sense of pardon brings surprise, then heartfelt regret, and next, it creates intense love in us. "We love because he first loved us." We love him best of all because he pardoned us. No one loves God as much as the man or woman who has had much forgiven. The Bible tells us about the woman who washed the Savior's "feet with her tears and wiped them with the hair of her head." When the Pharisee, whose guest he was, objected, Jesus replied, "I tell you, her sins, which are many, are forgiven—for she loved much. But he who is forgiven little, loves little."

Ordinary Christians have never experienced any deep sense of sin, and as a result, Christ is a very ordinary Savior to them. Ah, but when a man feels he is a wicked sinner and that he should have been in hell, and in the hottest part of it, if it had not been for sovereign grace, I tell you, if the Lord lifts that man up out of the pit and gives him a place among his servants, that is the man who will feel the tears in his eyes when he talks about the Savior's grace. That man cannot speak about redeeming grace and dying love without feeling a charming music in those precious words, the best and most precious music in the world. The more wicked the sinner the more love they have for the Lord when they are forgiven. To the extent they feel their sin, to the same extent they love their Redeemer.

The old saying goes, "The burnt child dreads the fire." I will tell you the child that dreads the fire the most. If there could be a child that had burned itself in the fire, and then all its sores and blisters were taken off itself and laid on its mother, and that child saw his mother's face all scarred and marred with the burning and saw her body in pain on her dear child's account, I am sure the child would hate all idea of playing with fire as long as it lived. Many suffer for sin personally, but do not hate it. They will go back to the very sin that injured them, like moths fly again to the candle. But to see someone else suffering for my faults, Immanuel, God with us, to see his hands nailed to the cross, and his feet pierced, and his heart gashed, and all his life flowing out in blood, and bearing unimaginable agonies for my sins, makes me curse the very name of sin and I absolutely hate it. We want to be perfect. We long and sigh and cry to be delivered from everything that has one murderous spot of the Savior's blood on it. If that knife over there had been used to kill your friend, would you treasure it and think about that deadly device a lot? Sin killed Jesus! Sin killed Jesus! Away with it! Away with it! My precious Christ was murdered by sin! From now on I am dead to sin! This is the spirit that divine grace breeds in every Christian. The more certain they are of their pardon, the more intensely, by God's grace, they hate their sin. Our gospel is a reforming gospel, a sanctifying gospel. It is a gospel that delivers people from the power of sin and brings them, through the power of love, into the blessed liberty of the children of God.

In closing, I share the following story. It represents the condition of every unconverted person before God. Many years ago in Russia a regiment of troops mutinied. They were at some distance from the capital and were so furious that they murdered their officers and resolved never to submit to discipline. But the emperor, who was a very wise and discerning man, no sooner heard of it than, all alone and unattended, he went into the barracks where the men were. He spoke sternly to them. He said, "Soldiers, you have committed such offense against the law that every one of you deserves to be put to death. There is no hope of mercy for any of you unless you lay down your arms immediately, and surrender to me, your emperor, come what may." And they did it. They immediately threw down their arms and surrendered even with the heads of their officers lying at their feet. The emperor said at once, "Men, I pardon you. You will be the bravest troops I ever had." And they were.

That is just what God says to the sinner. "Now, sinner, you have done what deserves my wrath. Down with your weapons of rebellion! Throw down your arms immediately. I will not talk with you until you submit to my sovereign authority." And then he says, "Believe in my Son. Trust him. Accept him as your Savior. If you do this, you are forgiven, and from now on you will be the most loving creatures that my hands have made. You will love me better than the angels, because even though they never sinned, they never had a God become an angel, and bleed and die for them. You know what sin is and will hate it. You know what goodness is, because you have seen it in my Son, and from this point on you will fight to be like him. Your grateful songs will be among the sweetest notes that will come up to my throne."

> Blessings forever on the Lamb,
> Who bore the curse for wretched men!
> Let angels sound his sacred name,
> And every creature say, "Amen!"

No one will sing the praises of God more loudly than those who have been washed in the precious blood and have had their transgressions blotted out.

The Lord bless you and give every one of you to know and taste this, and at this very hour, too, if it is his will, for Jesus' sake! Amen.

WHERE ARE YOU GOING?

A Sermon Delivered on Sunday Morning, August 4, 1889
by C. H. Spurgeon
at the Metropolitan Tabernacle, London

Job 23:10

But he knows the way that I take; when he has tried me, I shall come out as gold.

Introduction

I have used our past few Sunday mornings together to instruct the people of God to improve their walk with their Lord. However, it would not be right for me to continue that way without a break. I am a fisher of men as well as a shepherd of the flock. I must pay attention to both offices. There are souls here who are perishing, sinners needing to be saved by Christ. Therefore I must leave the flock and go after the wanderers. I must lay down the crook of the shepherd and take up the net of the fisherman. My aim today is to persuade the careless. This will be a simple sermon, full of serious reasoning. My aim at this moment is not so much to explain doctrine as to stir up hearts. Oh, for the power of the Holy Spirit, without which my goal would fail completely! We have been praying this morning for the conversion of many and we expect our prayers to be heard. The question is not, Will any be converted through this sermon? but, Who will it be? Many have come here with no higher motive than to see the great congregation and hear the preacher. We trust many of them will be met with God's infinite mercy and find the way to eternal life. May this be the spiritual birthday of many, a day to be remembered by them throughout eternity!

Job could not understand why God was treating him the way he was. He had lost his possessions, then his children, and finally, his health. He was greatly confused. He could not find the Lord who, until now, had been his constant companion. Job cries, "Behold, I go forward, but he is not there, and backward, but I do not perceive him; on the left hand when he is working, I do not behold him; he turns to the right hand, but I do not see him." But if Job did not know the way of the Lord, the Lord knew Job's way. It is a great comfort that, when we cannot see the Lord, he sees us and is aware of what is happening to us. It is not so important that we understand what the Lord is doing as that the Lord understands what we are doing. The great fact that he does understand our situation should make a great impression on us. Our circumstances may be far beyond our ability to grasp, but they are plain to him who sees the end from the beginning and understands the secrets of all hearts.

Because God knew Job's situation, Job could turn from the unfair judgments of his unfeeling friends and appeal to the Lord God himself. He pleaded in the supreme court, where his case was known, and refused the verdicts of mistaken men. "Whoever does what is true comes to the light." Job knew that light was with God, so he hurried to that light, so his deeds could be clearly seen. Like a bird that signals the return of the morning, Job could sing when he stood in the light of God. He was glad the Lord knew the way he took, and knew his motives and desires. That knowledge brought him to the conclusion that he would be helped in his trials and brought safely through them. "When he has tried me, I shall come out as gold."

These words provide rich comfort to the saints. If I were to use them for that purpose this morning, I would expect the Lord's people to rejoice, knowing the observant eye and gracious thoughts of the Lord are always on them. Our entire condition lies open to "him to whom we must give account." Though we may never be understood by men, we are always understood by our God.

> "'Tis no surprising thing
> That we should be unknown:
> The Jewish world knew not their King,
> God's everlasting Son."

As the Son of God was known to the Father, though unknown to all the world, so we are hidden from the knowledge of men, but well known by the Most High. "The Lord knows those who are his." "You have seen my affliction; you have known the distress of my soul."

But I cannot use this time to comfort the people of God. There is more urgent work to do; we must awaken the unconverted. Their way is evil and "its end is the way to death." Oh, that I could stir them up to a sense of their condition! With that in mind, I will ask four questions of every person within the sound of my voice. God knows the way you take. I will ask you first: *Do you know your own way?* Second: *Is it a comfort to you that God knows your way?* Third: *Are you tried in the way?* And if so, finally: *Do you have confidence in God for the result of that trial?* Can you say with Job, "When he has tried me, I shall come out as gold"?

Do You Know Your Own Way?

I will first ask my hearer, DO YOU KNOW YOUR OWN WAY? You do have a direction. There is a way you have taken, chosen, selected for yourself. There is a way you follow in desire, word and action. As far as your life is left to your own choosing, there is a way you take voluntarily and follow willingly. Do you know what that way is? Not everyone knows even that much. It is a very simple question, but a very needful one, because many walk on as if in a dream.

Do you know where you are going? "Of course," says one, "everybody knows where they are going." Do *you* know where *you* are going? And, do you carefully consider where that will take you? You are steaming across the deep sea of time and into the main ocean of eternity, to what port are you steering? Where are you going? The birds know their time and place when they fly away in due season, but do you know to where you are speeding? Do you keep a look out, looking for the shore? What shore are you expecting to see? What is your purpose in living? What is the reason and direction of your daily life?

I am afraid that many in this vast congregation are not prepared to give a direct answer that would be pleasant to talk about or even think about. Is this not strange? If I were going out to sea tomorrow, I would not walk on board a ship and then ask, "Where are you going?" The captain would think I was crazy if I embarked before I knew where the vessel was going. I first make up my mind where I will go and then select a ship that is likely to get me there safely and comfortably. You must know where you are going. The most important thing with the captain of a ship is getting his ship safely into the port for which it is headed. That goal overrules everything else. Getting into port is the thought of every watch, every glance at the chart, every check of the instruments. The captain's heart is set on reaching his destination. His hope is to arrive there safely and he knows where he is headed. He would not expect to get there if he had not decided to go there. How is it with you, dear friend? You are speeding toward heaven or hell. Which of these is your port? I know of no final home for souls except the brightness of the Father's glory or the darkness of Jehovah's wrath. At which of these will you end up? Which way are you intentionally going? What is it you are aiming at?

Are you living for God? Or, are you living in such a way that the result must be eternal banishment from his presence?

Surely, to insist on an answer does not require fine words to coax you. The question is vital to your happiness. Your own self-interest should persuade you to consider it. I will not use an analogy or illustration, because I am not here to please, but to get you to consider your destination. This is a question for every man and woman in this building. Where are you going? Where will the life you are now leading bring you in the end? Do not dismiss this question. It is not disrespectful and it is not unnecessary. I call on you to answer in the name of the Lord.

If you will answer that question, allow me to ask another. Do you know *how* you are going? In whose strength are you proceeding on your journey? If you feel you can truthfully say, "I am seeking that which is right and good," then I strongly urge you to honestly answer, Who are you depending on to get you there? Are you relying on your own power, or have you received strength from on high? Is your hope in your own decisions and strength, or have you received help from the Spirit of God? Remember, there are days in every life-voyage when the storm-fiend throws all human power into confusion. We are likely to run into rocks or sandbars in even the fairest weather, but the voyage of life is rarely without its gales and hurricanes. We must be prepared for violent windy storms. Our own unaided strength will not endure the waves and winds of the ocean of life. If you are trusting in yourself, disaster will overtake you. The Lord brings people to their desired port; but left to themselves, they are no match for the thousand dangers of their mysterious voyage.

Is God with you? Has the Lord Jesus become your strength and your song? Do you sail under the flag of the blood-red Cross? If you are trusting in the Lord alone, then disappointment, failure, and shipwreck are impossible. But if you are hurrying along without God as your Guide and Protector, then your weakness and folly will be made clear before long, to your inevitable ruin. You may push on full steam ahead into the teeth of the wind, but it will be all in vain; you will never reach the Port of Heaven.

Are there any here who brush my question aside? Do you refuse to tell us where you are going? When a great ship is crossing the sea and comes within sight of another ship, they ask, "What is your destination?" If the other vessel paid no attention and gave no answer whatever, it would look suspicious. A craft that will not say where it is going! We don't like the look of it. If a naval ship were in the area, and challenged a vessel, and received no response to the question, "To what port are you headed?" I think they would fire a shot across her bow and make her heave to, until she did answer. Might the silent craft not prove to be a pirate?

When a man confesses that he does not know where he is going, or what business he is up to, the police officer concludes that he is probably going somewhere he should not or is up to something he should not be. If you are afraid to think about your future, your fear is a bad sign. The shopkeeper who is afraid to look into his accounts will have them looked into by an officer from the Bankruptcy Court before long. He who does not dare to look at his own face in the mirror must be an ugly fellow. You who dare not examine your own characters, have bad characters. Not know where you are going! Ah me! Do you wish to all of a sudden find yourselves in hell? Will you find yourself, like the rich man in Jesus' parable, lifting up your eyes to hopeless misery?

I am suspicious of you who cannot tell where you are going; and I wish you would be suspicious of yourselves. You who do not like self-examination are the people who need it most. You who shun awkward questions are the very people who need to face them. I usually speak out—pretty plainly. Those of you who are used to me are not angry, but sometimes visitors are offended and say that they will not tolerate being spoken to like that. Ah, my friend! Your unfriendly mood shows you are in a bad way and do not wish to be corrected. If you honestly desired to be set right, you would appreciate straight talk and honest rebukes. Do you prefer to go to a doctor who has a reputation for saying, "There is not much the matter with you. A little change of air, a mild sedative, and you will soon be just fine"? No; the wise person wants to know the truth, no matter how alarming that truth may be. The person who is honest and hopeful wants a thorough examination, and invites the preacher to speak to him truthfully, even if the result causes him distress. If you refuse to answer where you are going, it is because you are going down to the pit. If you will not answer the question, "Where are you going?" I fear your way is one that you cannot defend, a way that will end in endless sorrow.

Is anyone here forced to admit, "I have chosen the evil road"? Remember, the Lord knows the way you take. I am concerned for you to know the truth about your situation and future. I tremble about you continuing in your ignorance. I wish every person here who is serving Satan would be aware of what they are doing. "If the Lord is God, follow him; but if Baal, then follow him." Be wholehearted one way or the other. If you have chosen the service of sin, own up to it, at least to yourself. Choose your way of life in broad daylight. If you intend to die without hope in Christ, say so. If you are determined to let the future happen come what may, and take any risk, then put your daring resolution down in black and white. If you believe you will die like a dog and see no hereafter, do not hide your shame from yourself, be true to your own choice. If you choose the way of evil pleasures, do it deliberately after weighing everything that can be said on the other side.

But there is this comfort to me, even if you have chosen the wrong way— your choice does not need to be permanent. The grace of God can come in and lead you to immediately reverse your course. I hope you will say, "I had not thought of that, but I am certainly going in the wrong direction, and, God helping me, I will not go an inch further!" The past can be forgiven through our Lord Jesus Christ. The present and the future can be changed by the power of the Holy Spirit. The grace of God can lead you to turn away from that which you have eagerly followed and cause you to seek after that which you have rejected. Oh, that your cry today might be, "Holiness and heaven!" You have not been on the Lord's side up to now, but you can enlist in the army of the Lord Jesus this moment. I would gladly stop your vessel in her evil voyage. I am firing a shot across your bow. My serious warning to you is, consider your ways. Think about it; where are you going? Break off your sins and replace them with righteousness. It is time to seek the Lord. "Turn back, turn back from your evil ways, for why will you die?" This is the voice of God's own Word to you. Hear it, and accept this counsel, and, God helping you, change course now.

My friend, perhaps you are adrift. Do you say, "I am not definitely sailing for heaven, but neither am I determined to steer in the other direction. I do not quite know what to say about myself"? Are you drifting? Are you like a ship left to the mercy of the winds and waves? This is a shameful condition, a dangerous place to be! What! Are you nothing more than a log floating on the water? I would not like to be a passenger in a ship that had no course plotted on the chart, no pilot at the helm, no one on watch. Surely, you are waterlogged if not falling apart, you will be totally wrecked before long. Your outlook is dark!

Some time ago, I read in a paper about a gentleman brought up before the judge. What was the charge against him? You will not think it very serious. He was found wandering in the fields. He was asked where he was going. He said he was not going anywhere. He was asked where he came from. He said he did now know. They asked him where his home was. He said he had none. What did they charge him with? For being a psychopath! The man who has no aim or goal in life, but just wanders about anywhere or nowhere, acts like a dangerous madman, and is certainly not mentally stable.

What! Am I aiming at nothing? Do I have all this machinery of life, a body and soul more wonderful than the finest luxury liner, and am I going nowhere? My heartbeats are the pulsing of a divinely built machine. Does it live for nothing? Do I get up every morning, and go about this world, and work hard, all for nothing that will last? As a being created by God for the noblest purposes, am I spending my existence with no purpose? How foolish! Why, surely, like the Prodigal Son, I need to wake up and ask myself, Can it be right for me to waste the precious gifts of time, and life, and power? If I were nothing, it would make sense that I aim at nothing. But, as a human being, I should have a high purpose and pursue it energetically. Do not say you are drifting. It is a terrible answer. It implies awful danger and throws suspicion on your sanity. If you have reason, use it in a reasonable way. Do not play the fool.

Can you say, "Yes, I am heading for the right port"? It may be that your voice is trembling with a holy fear, but nevertheless I am glad to hear you say it. I rejoice if you can say, "Christ commands me, I am trusting to his guidance. He is my way, my life, my end." I congratulate you, dear friend. We will sail together, as God helps us, under the convoy of our Lord Jesus, who is the Fleet Admiral of the sea of life. We will stay with his fleet until we drop anchor in the glassy sea. But now that you know your way and are assured that you are on the right course, full speed ahead. Apply yourself to the work to which you have dedicated yourself. Do not waste a single moment. Do not allow your energy to sleep. Use every ability you possess. If you are serving the Lord, serve him with all your might. Is it not written, "You shall love the Lord your God with all your heart and with all your soul and with all your strength and with all your mind"? These words sound to me like great strokes of the soul's engine! They urge us to move forward in the holy voyage. Brothers and sisters, our life is a race, we must run in it. It must be hard running, too. "Let us also lay aside every weight, and sin which clings so closely, and let us run with endurance the race that is set before us." If we are really on the right course, let us move forward with all our powers; and may God help us so we can win the prize!

The first question is, Where are you going? Know for certain whose you are, where you are, and where you are going. Who do you belong to, where do you stand before God, and are you on the road to heaven or hell?

Are You Comfortable Knowing That God Knows Your Way?

ARE YOU COMFORTABLE KNOWING THAT GOD KNOWS YOUR WAY? Seriously, I believe that one of the best tests of human character is how we react to the great truth that God knows and sees everything. If it bothers you that God sees you, then it *should* bother you. If you are delighted that God sees you, then you may reasonably conclude there is something right and true in your heart, something that God approves. You are among those who live the truth, because you come to the light and cry, "Search me, O God." Allow me to apply the test to you, by asking what you think of the fact that the Lord knows you completely. Remember, if your heart condemns you, God is greater than your heart and knows all things; but if your heart does not condemn you, then you have confidence toward God.

"He knows the way that I take." Dear friend, God absolutely knows the way you take. The Hebrew may be read, "He knows the way that is in me." I gather from this that the Lord not only knows our outward actions, but our inward feelings. He know our likes and dislikes, our desires and our plans, our imaginations and tendencies. He not only knows what we do, but what we would do if we could. He knows the way we would go if the restraints of society and the fear of consequences were removed; and that, perhaps, is a more important indicator of our character than the actions of which we are actually guilty. God knows what you think about, what you wish for, and what pleases you. He not only knows the surface-tint of your character, but the core secrets of your heart. The Lord knows you completely. Think about that. Does it bring you any joy, this morning, to think that the Lord reads all the secrets of your heart? Whether you rejoice over that or not, that is the way it is and ever will be.

The Lord knows you and approves if you follow the way that is right. "He knows those who take refuge in him." That is, he approves them. If there is in you even a faint desire to please God, he knows it and looks on it with pleasure. If you are in the habit of having private prayer, if you do good anonymously, if you conquer evil passions, if you honor God by patience, if you present gifts to him that nobody ever hears about, he knows it all, and he smiles over it. Does this give you pleasure? Greater pleasure than if others praised you for it? Then it is well with you. But if you put the praise of others before the approval of God, you are in an evil condition. If you can say this morning, "I am glad God knows what I do, his approval is heaven to me," then know there is a work of grace in your heart and that you are a follower of Jesus.

God knows your way, no matter how falsely others may represent you. Those three men who looked on Job so skeptically, who accused him of being a hypocrite, and of practicing evil in secret; Job could answer them, "The Lord knows the way that I take." Are you the victim of slander? The Lord knows the truth. If you have been sadly misunderstood, whether by ungenerous people who intentionally misrepresented you or by others who voiced their opinions without all the facts, God knows all about you; and his knowledge is more important that the opinions of dying people. If you are not afraid to put your character and profession of faith before the eye of the Lord, then you have little reason to be anxious, even when everyone calls you evil.

The Lord knows the way that you take, even if you have difficulty describing that way yourself. Some gracious people are like Moses, who was "slow of speech and of tongue," and have great difficulty saying anything about the matters of their soul. Coming to see the elders of the church is quite an unpleasant experience. I am half afraid they even feel it is a trial to see me, poor creature that I am. They are timid in speech, though they would be bold in act. They could die for Jesus, but they find it hard to speak for him. Their heart is right, but when they begin to talk, their tongue fails them. They are not able to describe their conversion even though they feel it. They love repentance, but can barely describe their own repenting. They have believed in the Lord Jesus, but it would bewilder them to attempt to explain what faith is. Trembling one, fall back on this: "He knows the way that I take." Even if I cannot communicate my faith, he still accepts it. If I cannot describe his work in my soul, he still recognizes the work of his own hands.

Another great mercy is that God knows the way we take when we hardly know it ourselves. There are times with the true children of God when they cannot see their way, nor even take their bearings. It is not every saint that knows their longitude and latitude. It is not every saint that is sure they are a saint. We have to ask, "Is my repentance real? Is my faith true? Have I really passed from death to life? Am I really the Lord's?" I do not wish for you to be in such a condition. It is a pity that such a question is even possible; but I know many sincere saints often question their salvation, and not without reason. Here is comfort: The Lord knows his children. He knows grace is in them, he knows their precious faith, and their desire for heaven, he knows because he is the author and creator of all of them. He knows his own work and cannot be tricked. Dear friends, for that reason, let us feel confident that God knows us better than we know ourselves and his verdict is more accurate than even our conscience.

I remind you again, God knows your way at this very moment. He not only knows the way you have taken and the way you will take, but the way you are choosing for yourself right now. He knows how you are responding to this sermon you are hearing. You may have decided this preacher is very tiresome. I can accept that, but the subject is still one you ought to consider, so please bear with me. But if you are thinking, "No, it is not that; but I do not want to be probed and questioned like this." The Lord knows you are resisting his Spirit and hardening your heart against his rebuke. Are you comfortable with that? I think I hear someone say, "I really wish to be right, but I am afraid I am not right. Oh, that I could be made right before God." God knows that feeling. Make that your prayer and whisper it in his ear. If you can say, "I am willing to be challenged, I know the port I am headed for, I am not a pirate, I am headed for the New Jerusalem," then I rejoice. The Lord knows. He looks on your thoughts, your wishes, and your determination with fondness. He knows your heart. Does that give you comfort? It should! But if it saddens you that God knows your present condition, then you should be afraid, because there is something about you that you should fear. Adam knew he was naked and sewed fig leaves together to hide himself from God and the person who tries to hide themself from God is also afraid because of their nakedness. If they were clothed in the righteousness of the Lord Jesus, they would have no reason to try to hide. They would be willing to not only examine themself, but to be examined by the Lord.

Do You Meet with Trials Along the Way?

I have handled two questions: Do you know where you are going? Are you comfortable knowing that God knows where you are going?

My third question is, DO YOU MEET WITH TRIALS ALONG THE WAY? I anticipate your answer. Of the thousands here this morning, not one has been completely free from sorrow. I think I hear someone saying, "Pastor, I have had more trouble since I have been a Christian than I ever had before." I met with just such a case the other day. A man said to me, "I never went to a place of worship for many years and I always seemed to prosper. I finally began to think about divine things and attend the house of God, but since then I have had nothing but trouble." He was not complaining about God, but he did think it was very strange. Friend, please listen to me. These troubles are no sign that you are on the wrong course. Job was in the right way and the Lord knew it; and yet he permitted Job to be fiercely tried.

There are trials in all ways. Even the road to destruction, wide as it is, has no path that avoids trials. Some sinners go over hedge and ditch to hell. If a man is determined to live for this world, he will not find the paths of sin to be paths of peace. The wicked may be uncomfortable; God opposes them because they oppose him. No one, whether they rule a country, or are part of the middle-class, or barely eke out a living can live without affliction. There are troubles in a cottage near the forest as well as in a palace by the sea. "Man is born to trouble." If you look for a world without thorns and thistles, you will not find it here.

Remember, too, the very greatest of the saints have been afflicted. The Bible records the lives of believers. Can you remember the life of a single believer who lived and died without sorrow? I cannot. Start with father Abraham. The Lord tested Abraham. Go on to Moses, a king in Israel. Did he not have many trials, heavy ones? Remember David and all his affliction. Come down to New Testament times. The apostles were so tried that one of them said, "If in this life only we have hoped in Christ, we are of all people most to be pitied." They reached their rest through a great deal of tribulation. If the saints of God acknowledged that their way was full of difficulty, then you must not assume you are on the wrong road because you meet with trials. Is there any ocean on which a ship can sail without danger of storms? Where there is a sea there may be storms, and where there is life there will be changes, temptations, difficulties and sorrows.

Trials come from God and trials are no evidence that God is not with us. Job says, "When he has tried me." He sees the hand of God in his afflictions. The devil caused the trouble, but the Lord not only permitted it, he had a purpose in it. Without God agreeing to it, none of Job's afflictions could have happened. It was God who tried Job and it is God who tries us. No trouble comes to us without divine permission. All the dogs of affliction are muzzled until God sets them loose. A dog may not even bark at a child of God unless God permits it. Troubles do not spring out of the ground like weeds growing in a haphazard way, but like plants organized in the garden. God appoints the weight and number of all our troubles. If he declares the number will be ten, there cannot be eleven. If he wills to burden us with a certain weight, no one can add half an ounce more. Since every trial comes from God, afflictions are no proof that you are out of God's way.

According to the text, these trials are tests: "When he has tried me." The trials that came to Job were evidence that he was real and sincere. Did not the enemy say, "Have you not put a hedge around him and his house and all that he has, on every side? You have blessed the work of his hands, and his possessions have increased in the land. But stretch out your hand and touch all that he has, and he will curse you to your face." The devil claims we will follow God for what we can get out of him, like dogs follow men for bones. The Lord lets the devil see that our love is not bought by materials things. We are not greedy followers, but loving children of the Lord who will cry out under terrible suffering, "Though he slay me, I will hope in him." Our sincerity is made known by our endurance of grief. It proves we are not mere pretenders, but true heirs of God.

When you meet with troubles, remember they will come to an end. That holy man in our text says, "When he has tried me." As much as to say, he will not always be trying us. There will come a time when he will have finished trying me. Beloved, put a brave heart to a steep hill and you will climb it before long. Put the ship in good trim for a storm; and though the winds may howl for a while, they will eventually sob themselves to sleep. There is a sea of glass for us after the sea of storms. Have patience, the end will come. Many a man of God has lived through a hundred troubles when he thought just one would kill him and you will experience the same.

You young beginners, you who have only recently set out on your journey to the kingdom, do not be blown away if you meet with conflicts; do not be surprised if you meet with difficulties early in your voyage. Let your trials be proof that you are in the right way, rather than the wrong way; "for what son is there whom his father does not discipline?" The person on his way to hell will find many to help him on the way, but the person on his way to heaven may need to fight his way through an army of troubles. Take courage. The rod is one of the signs of being a child of God. If you were not God's child, then you might be left undisciplined. But because you are dear to him, he will whip you when you disobey. If you were only a bit of common clay God would not put you into the furnace. But because you are gold and he knows it, you must be refined. Refining is needed, therefore you must be tested by fire. Those who are headed for heaven will meet with storms on their voyage to glory.

Do You Have Confidence in God When These Storms Come?

Can you say with Job, "When he has tried me, I shall come out as gold"? If you are really trusting in Jesus, if he is everything to you, you may say this with confidence, because you will know every word is true. If you have really given yourself up to being saved by grace, do not hesitate to believe that you will arrive safely at last. I do not like people coming to Christ and trusting him with only a temporary faith as if he would only keep them safe for a day or two, but could not protect them all their lives. TRUST CHRIST FOR EVERLASTING SALVATION. Note that word "everlasting." I thank God, that when I believed in his Son Jesus Christ, he gave me the grace to firmly believe it was forever. I believed that he who began a good work in me would bring it to completion at the day of Jesus Christ. I believed in the Lord Jesus, not for a year or two, but for all the days of my life, and to eternity. I want your faith to be like that and grasp the Lord as your Savior to the utmost.

I do not know what troubles may come, nor what temptations may surface; but I know in whose hands I am, and I am persuaded that he is able to care for me, so that "when he has tried me, I shall come out as gold." I will go into the fire, but I will not be burned up in it. "I shall come out." Like the three holy children, though the furnace is heated seven times hotter, yet the Son of man will be with me in the furnace, and "I shall come out" with not even the smell of fire on me. Yes, "I shall come out," and no one can stop me. It is good to begin with this holy confidence and let that confidence increase as you get closer to the final reward. Has God not promised that we will never perish? Will we not, therefore, come out as gold?

This confidence is based on the Lord's knowledge of us. "He knows the way that I take," therefore, "When he has tried me, I will come out as gold." If something could happen to us that the Lord had not foreseen and provided for, we might be in great danger. But he knows our way even to the finish and has prepared for the rough places. If some amazing calamity could come upon us on which the Lord had not counted, we might well be afraid of being shipwrecked. But our Lord's foreseeing eye has swept the horizon and prepared us for all weathers. He knows where storms lie in wait and cyclones hide. He is at home managing tempests and tornadoes. If his farseeing eye has spied out a long sickness for us and a gradual and painful death, then he has prepared whatever is necessary to take us through it. If he has looked into the mysterious unknown of the apocalyptic revelation and seen unimaginable horrors and terrors that would melt the heart, he has already anticipated and prepared for them. It is enough for us that our Father knows what we need and that, "When he has tried us, we will come out as gold."

This confidence must be maintained by genuineness. If someone is not sure they are genuine, they cannot have confidence in God. If you are a bit of gold and know it, the fire and you are friends. You will come out of it, because no fire will burn up gold. But if you suspect that you are some imitation metal, some rock that glitters but is not gold, then you will hate fire, and have nothing good to say about it. You will proudly grumble at the trials God brings. Why should you be tried? You will kick against God's hand if you are a hypocrite. But if you are really genuine, you will submit to whatever he brings and not lie down in despair. The motto of pure gold, is, "I will come out." Make that your hopeful confidence in the day of trouble. I want you to have this sense of genuineness that makes you know that you are what you profess to be, that you will also have the conviction that you will come out of every possible trial. I will be tempted, but "I will come out." I will be attacked by slander, but "I will come out." Be of good cheer. Oh gold, if you go into the fire as gold, you will come out as gold!

Again, Job says, "I shall come out as gold." It comes out proved. It has been tested and is now documented to be pure. And so will you. After the trial you will be able to say, "I now know I fear God, I now know that God is with me, strengthening me. I now see that he has helped me and I am sure I am his." How does gold come out of the furnace? It comes out purified. A lump of ore may not be as big as when it went into the fire, but it is quite precious. There is just as much gold in it now as there was at first. What is gone? Nothing except that which should be gone. The impurities are gone, but all the gold is still there. Oh child of God, you may decrease in size, but not in value! You may lose importance in this world, but not innocence. You may not talk so big, but there really will be more to talk about. And what gain it is to lose dross, to lose the worthless part of the ore! What gain to lose pride! What gain to lose self-sufficiency! What gain to lose all those tendencies to brag. You may thank God for your trials, because you will come out as gold purified.

How does gold come out of the furnace? It comes out ready for use. The goldsmith may take it and make what he pleases with it. It has been through the fire and the dross has been removed. It is ready to use. If you are on the way to heaven and you meet with difficulties, they will prepare you for higher service. You will be a more useful man; you will be a woman whom God can use more fully to comfort others who are full of sorrow. Spiritual afflictions are heavenly promotions. You are rising to a higher rank. You were only a corporal, but now God is making you a sergeant. Do not be discouraged. You that have set out for heaven this morning, do not go back because you get a rainy day when you start. Do not be like John Bunyan's Pliable. When he got to the Slough of Despond, and tumbled in, all he did was struggle to get out on the side nearest to where he began his journey. He said, "If I may only once get out of this bog, you may have that grand city for yourself." Come, be like Christian, who, even though he sank, always kept his face in the right direction and always turned his back to the City of Destruction. "No," he said, "if I sink in deep mire where there is no place to stand, I will go down with my eyes toward the hills where my help comes from." "I am bound for the Promised Land, and if all my enemies stand in the way as one great army, I will die with my face toward the New Jerusalem. I will, God helping me, continue to hold on to the very end." May the Lord bless you. He knows the way you take; and when he has tried you, he will bring you out as gold. Amen.

JESUS THE WAY

A Sermon Delivered on a Sunday Evening in 1862
by C. H. Spurgeon at the Metropolitan Tabernacle, London

John 14:3-7

"And if I go and prepare a place for you, I will come again and will take you to myself, that where I am you may be also. And you know the way to where I am going." Thomas said to him, "Lord, we do not know where you are going. How can we know the way?" Jesus said to him, "**I am the way**, and the truth, and the life. No one comes to the Father except through me. If you had known me, you would have known my Father also. From now on you do know him and have seen him."

Introduction

It is getting dark and we are lost in the mountains. There is an awful cliff nearby, a quarter of a mile straight down. There is also a quagmire in the area, and if someone wanders into it, they will never get out. There is a forest not far away and if someone should be lost in its twisted paths, they will certainly not find their way before sunrise. What do we need? Why, we need someone who will tell us the way!

Our friend the philosopher, with whom we talked half-an-hour ago, was very helpful to us then and gave us a great deal of information. But he does not know the way. Right now, we would rather have the poorest boy that feeds the sheep on the hills for a companion than that man. The classic scholar, who has been repeating masterly lines from Horace and delighting us with admirable quotations from Virgil, was a fine person to be with while we could see our path and had hope of reaching our home by nightfall. But now the poorest girl with uncombed hair who can just point the way to a place where we may rest tonight will be of more value to us. What we need is to know the way!

Dear Friends, this is the case with poor fallen humanity. The need of mankind is not the refined lecture of the learned, nor the sharp skill of the debater. We simply need someone to show us the way! The most precious person you and I have seen, or ever will see, will be the person who will be blessed and honored of God to us to say, "Behold the way to God, to life, to salvation and to heaven." I have no reason to apologize for coming out again today to show the way. There are many here who are lost and there are some on whom the shadows of night are falling. Their hair is gray, they gasp for air as they walk and lean on their cane to support their wobbling legs. Their case is dangerous. They cannot discover the pathway. Surely they will listen to any voice, from any person, however rough he may be, if they can only discover what is the way to eternal life!

We were traveling some time ago when the driver, as it was getting nearly dark, informed us that he had never been on that road before. One can hardly describe how pleased we were to see a road sign. Now, a road sign is not a very interesting thing; there is nothing very poetical about it. It may be questionable whether it decorates the road as it points out the way with only a word or two painted on it. However near nightfall, when neither the driver nor you know the way, it is about the most pleasant thing you meet! I will stand here tonight as a simple road sign. The words may be dry, but it will be enough for you if they are clear enough to show you the way! Mr. William Jay tells us that one time, when riding on the mail coach along the rolling countryside to the town of Bath, he asked the coachman a great many questions. He asked, "Whose home is that? What squire owns the fine lawn? And what gentleman is the squire of that estate over there?" The driver answered all his questions with, "I don't know. I don't know." At last, Mr. Jay said to him, "Well, what do you know?" "Why," he said, "I know how to drive you to Bath." Well, now, I do not pretend to have any more knowledge than this—I do know the way to heaven and I do hope I will be able to tell it to you so plainly and so simply that some here who are lost, as in a wild forest, may see the path and, by grace, they will to run to it!

The Way Is Unique

First, let us notice THE EXCLUSIVENESS OF OUR TEXT. "I am the way."

Christ declares that he, and only he, is the way to peace with God, to pardon, to righteousness and to heaven! Lies may tolerate lies, but truth never can. Two lies can live in the same house and never quarrel, but truth cannot endure a lie even if it lives in the highest part of the attic! Truth has sworn war to the death against falsehood and will never tolerate a lie. The Hindu meets the Muslim and says, "You are no doubt as sincere as we are, and you and we will meet in the right place at the last." They would greet the Christian, too, and say the same to him, but it is a necessity, if our religion is true, that it should reject every other religion and that it should say to those who do not know Christ, "No one can lay a foundation other than that which is laid, which is Jesus Christ." Yes, it goes even further and pronounces its curse on those who claim there is any other way! "Even if we or an angel from heaven should preach to you a gospel contrary to the one we preached to you, let him be accursed." I only mention these other ways to assure you, in God's name, that there are roads that lead to hell, but none of them can bring you to heaven. There is only one way that the soul can come to God and find eternal life—and that way is Christ!

I see humanity as lost in a great wilderness. There are no paths. Suddenly before the sad eyes of the lost travelers, an old woman appears whose hand is blood red and her eyes are flashing fire. She points and says, "Lost people, this is the way." What is that before our eyes? I see an unstoppable force rolling through the way, a juggernaut crushing flesh and bones with every revolution of its wheels. In its wake there stands a monument to superstition! The old woman points to it and tells the mother to take her child and throw her dear one into the Ganges River. "This is the way," says the foul witch of Superstition. "This is the way to come to God." We denounce her! In God's name, we denounce her as a demon escaped from hell! "Shall I give my firstborn for my transgression, the fruit of my body for the sin of my soul?" No, no! God detests such a sacrifice! You cannot reasonably think that what God hates can be acceptable to him! How can what you cannot bear to see be delightful to the Lord? No, brothers and sisters, God does not ask us to cut our flesh or starve ourselves. He is not pleased if we punish ourselves by wearing hair shirts or go about half naked. These do not please him, they only weary him.

If you wish to please God in some way invented by man, you are more likely to do it by being happy than by being miserable! Do you think that someone would please others by groans and sighs? I think not. How does self-torture please God? There is no such God in the Bible! All you nations of the East, turn from this cruel lie. This is not the way to heaven!

In our country we have deceivers who are more lovely than this old woman. False prophets are more likely to mislead you. Let me glance at some of the popular ways that claim to lead you to heaven, but will surely lead to hell. There is the way of good works. I thought we had distributed so many millions of tracts, preached so much in the streets and talked so long about people being saved by the blood of Christ and not by themselves, that really, the old fashioned heresy of self-righteousness would have been driven out of our land. But it still holds a strong position. When I get into conversation with people, I find, at all levels of society, there is still the same belief that people will go to heaven by what they did.

Someone said to me yesterday, "I suppose you sometimes feel discouraged." "Yes," I said, "I do." "Why," said he, "I should think the best men can sometimes hardly look back on their lives with pleasure and so they must feel a little afraid for the future." "Oh," I said, "if I had to look on my past life for my hope for the future, I would really be discouraged! Do you know that all my good works will not save me and that all the sins I have ever committed in the past will never damn me?" "No," he said, and he looked quite surprised at such a strange belief as that! The gospel teaches that when a person believes in Christ, the sin of the past is taken away and the righteousness of Christ is given in exchange. A person is not saved by what they, nor damned for who they were, but is saved through Jesus Christ and through Jesus Christ alone.

I was sitting in a boat not too long ago, and while the man was rowing me, I thought I would talk with him. He began to talk about various "new lights" that had sprung up in the village with their new thoughts about religion. People always pay more attention to these new "enlightened" opinions than they do about the sun itself. At length, the question came up of how he hoped to go to heaven. Well, he had raised eight children, he had never had any help from the church, he was an honest man and always helped his neighbors. When the cholera was spreading, he was about the only man in the village that would get up at night and run for the doctor. He felt that if he did not go to heaven it would not go well with most people. Yes, and I am afraid it will not go well with him either. That is, if that is all he is counting on!

I tell these two stories, taken from two different types of people, because I know we need to keep on exposing this old lie of Satan's that people are saved by their works. Those fig leaves that Adam wove together to cover his nakedness are still preferred by his descendants. They would rather go about trying to save themselves than accepting the robe of Christ's righteousness. A word or two with you, my friend. Do you say you will go to heaven by keeping the law of God? You have heard the old saying about locking the stable after the horse is gone. I am afraid it applies to you. So you are going to keep the stable shut now, and you are sure the horse will never get out? If you will go and look, you will find it is already out! How can you keep the law that you have already broken? If you want to be saved by keeping the law of God, remember the law of God is like a pure alabaster vase that must be presented to God without a crack or flaw. Do you not see that your vase is broken? There is a crack there! "Ah," you say, "that was a long time ago." Yes, I know it was, but it is still a crack. There is the black mark of your thumb just underneath there. Why, the vase is already broken, you cannot go to heaven by your good works when you have none! No, you have broken all God's commandments. Read the 20th chapter of Exodus. Read it through and see if there is a single commandment that you have not violated! I think you will soon find that from the first to the very last, you will be forced to cry, "I have sinned, oh Lord, and am condemned." You have already broken the law of God.

But then you will tell me that you have not broken it in public and that you have developed a great outward respect for it. Yes, but what does that matter if the inner heart is wrong? Even if someone could keep the outward letter of the law without a fault or mistake, yet, "we know that the law is spiritual" and it is impossible that any of the fallen race of Adam can keep it. No one can be saved by keeping the law.

I heard a story the other day that illustrates the way people make a distinction between inward and outward sin. A certain Sunday school superintendent happened to hear a girl crying after the other children had left. He went to her and asked her what she was crying about and she said, "The lady superintendent has kept me and has been talking to me about my dress. She says I should not dress so fine. I paid for it sir, and I have a right to wear it." The lady was called and after some discussion the superintendent (who was wise and sensible) sent the girl home. Now the lady herself was known for her fineness in dress. She was always very well dressed herself so, after the girl was gone, our friend put this question to her, "Miss So-and-So, you will excuse me, but did it never suggest itself to you that your own dress is rather fine?" "Yes," she said, "but then, that girl has flowers in her bonnet." Well," he said, "excuse me"—and he looked at her—"I think you have flowers in yours." "Ah, yes," she replied, "but do you not see, mine are inside my bonnet and hers are outside?"

Now, this is just how some people speak about sin. You condemn a man because he is such a sinner; you would not associate with such a great sinner! But if you would just look at yourselves, you would see that you are as great a sinner as he is. The only difference is you have blemishes of character on the inside and he has them outside! The truth is, sometimes the outside sinner is the less dishonorable of the two. Do you really think God makes such vain and empty distinctions as this? No, certainly not. Sin is sin. Whether it is inward or outward, it destroys you. Since you cannot keep the law inwardly why make so much effort to do the impossible?

This is not the way to heaven. Since Adam fell, no one has ever passed through the gate into everlasting life by works. Besides, even supposing that your past were wiped off your record, you cannot keep the law in the future; it is your nature to sin. It is such a basic part of you that it is certain you will violate the law. You have heard of the women who were ordered to fill a large tank with water and were told to bring the water in buckets that were full of holes. This is just what you are doing. You must fill the tremendous ocean of the law and your buckets are full of holes. Your nature, mend it as you may and repair it as you will, is still full of holes. Your pretended goodness will drip out drop by drop. More than that, your efforts to keep the law will be like water spilled on the ground that cannot be gathered up. Oh friends. I plead with you; do not seek to enter heaven by the works of the law. The Spirit says, "that a person is not justified by works of the law but through faith in Jesus Christ."

There is another guide who points another way. He calls himself *Sincere Obedience* and his way is just as popular, or rather more popular. This is how he puts it: "Well, if I cannot keep the whole law, yet I will trust to the mercy of God to make up for the rest. I have no doubt that what I do may go a great way and then the Lord Jesus Christ will make up the difference. I may be lacking a little, perhaps an ounce or two, but then the atonement will come in and the scale will be turned in my favor." Do you really think that Jesus Christ will ever partner with you to work out your salvation? "I have trodden the winepress alone, and from the peoples no one was with me." This is the triumphant shout of the Warrior as he comes back from Edom in garments red from the blood of his enemies. Do you think that, after that matchless speech, your puny voice will be heard saying, "But I was there; I did my part, I did what I could." No, even entertaining such a thought is sinning. You only bring a double curse on yourself by imagining that Christ will ever do part of the work and allow you to be his helper. Like the work of creation, salvation is by the Lord alone. From the beginning to the end it is not of man or by man.

There is another error, too, that is popular in certain areas and that is, *salvation by ceremonies.* We have it in the Church of Rome to this day. The priest pronounces certain hocus-pocuses and the thing is done. Other churches practice similar sleight of hand. They inform us we are nothing because we have not been properly ordained; we have no right to preach or lead a congregation. They are immediate descendants of the apostles. They are the honorable men. One touch of their finger, one sign of the cross, and a child of wrath instantly becomes "a member of Christ, a child of God, and an heir to the kingdom of heaven." True, the child may turn out to be a hardened criminal; but we are told that we should sincerely and without question believe that the infant's holy sprinkling made him a part of the body of Christ!

Do you believe it? Has the echo of John Wycliffe's voice, the Morning Star of the Reformation, died out to the point that those who would have us return to rituals and ceremonies for salvation will control our consciences? Will we whose heritage includes the Reformers and the glorious Puritans tolerate such teaching in our churches? Will we allow them to secretly enter into our churches with this false gospel? No! We say with Paul, "Even if we or an angel from heaven should preach to you a gospel contrary to the one we preached to you, let him be accursed."

Oliver Cromwell, before he became Lord Protector of the Commonwealth of England, once walked into the House of Commons and, putting down his hat, said, "I have just come from St. Paul's Cross, and I have heard a man there preach flat Popery." If Mr. Cromwell were here now, he might go into many of our churches and say the same about them. God has his ministers even in some of these churches. I trust, dear friends, that their earnest zeal will cause them to honestly protest this *salvation by ceremonies* and subdue this very popular delusion. You might as well hope to be saved by the mumblings of a witch as by the efforts of a priest. You might as well hope to enter heaven by crying out blasphemies as by a priest mumbling certain words that he thinks have saving power in them. Our God has repeatedly condemned those who delight in these errors, who keep back the blood of Jesus, and the power and value of his righteousness. I plead with you, do not think that this is the way to heaven. It is not! "Jesus said to him, 'I am the way.'"

I hardly need to mention any more of these old roads. Everyone seems to have one to travel on. One person gives so many dollars to charity, so it is well with him. Another intends to build homes for the poor, so it is well with her. Another is from a very respectable family and hopes he will not be sent down to hell with ordinary people. With one thing and another everyone thinks they will escape the wrath of God. I say to you again, if you have any hope except the one I am telling you about, it is a hope built on lies and will be swept away! May God sweep it away tonight and leave you bare and without any hope except that you may be led to accept Christ as the way, the only way, to heaven!

We may seem intolerant, we may seem to speak very harshly. But the price is too great for any mistake to be made. There is only one way to heaven and that way is Christ. The only way to walk in it is to simply, totally, and only trust in what Jesus Christ did on the cross, and what he does today by his prayers in heaven. Whoever does not come by this door will never come in at all. He who will not accept the yoke of Christ will not be accepted by God. Heaven has only one gate, and if you will not enter this way, "there no longer remains a sacrifice for sins, but a fearful expectation of judgment, and a fury of fire."

How is Jesus This Way?

Suppose that we have lost our way, and we meet a man, and ask him which is the way. He says, "I am the way." What does he mean? If he had said, I am the guide," I could understand that. But he says he is the way! Suppose he has a horse and carriage, and I ask him the way, and he says, "I am the way." No, you are the transportation along the way, not the way. I do not understand how you can be the way.

However, suppose I am near the sea where two areas of land become one during low tide and are divided by the incoming tide. The sand has been left bare by the receding tide and children sometimes go far out on those sands. The tide may suddenly return before they are aware of it and they are in danger of drowning. We are two children playing on the sands and suddenly we see that the sea has surrounded us in all directions and there is no possibility for us to get to land. Here comes a man on a noble horse. We cry to him, "Sir, which is the way of escape? He stoops down from his horse, lifts us up, and then says, "My children, I am the way." We can understand this perfectly. He is doing the work, fully, completely, entirely by himself. It becomes obvious that for him to say, "I am the way of escape for you" is entirely correct.

Or put it in another way. The house over there is on fire. There is a child up at the window desperately asking the way to escape the flames. A strong man lifts up his arms. All he wants the child to do is drop down, and let the man catch him, so he answers, "I am the way, my child; if you want to be rescued from the burning house, I am the way to be rescued."

If Christ only showed us the way to go, he could not say, "I am the way." But when he does it all from first to last, when he takes it completely out of our hands, and makes it his business from beginning to end, then it is no exaggeration for the Master to say, "I am the way." Let us put it clearly. You are in debt to God, sinner. You say, "How can I pay him? If I were to lie in the flames of hell and burn forever, I could not pay the debt." Christ replies, "I am the way," and he speaks the truth. He is the Payer and the payment! Sinner, if you believe on Christ now, he took your place, took your guilt, paid your debts, down to the last penny. If you are a believer, you are released from your debt. You owe nothing except to love God and be faithful to him.

But you tell me that I owe God perfect obedience. You do! Christ has obeyed perfectly and therefore he can say, "I am the way." He is the way to perfect obedience. He has kept the law, glorified it, and made it honorable. Accept the work he has finished and you will find that he is the way. Do you want to be a child of God tonight? Christ says, "I am the way." Be one with Christ, and then, because Christ is God's Son, you will be God's child also. Do you want peace with God? Trust Christ tonight, put your soul in Christ's hands; he is your Peace, he is also your way to peace. Do you wish to be saved tonight? Oh my dear hearers, are there not some of you who want to be saved tonight? Then Jesus says, "I am the way." Not merely the Savior, but the salvation. Trust Christ and you have salvation, because Christ says, "I am your salvation." Take him, and in taking him, you have the blood that washes, the robe that clothes, the medicine that heals, the jewels that decorate. You have the life that will last and the crown that will adorn. Christ is everything. All you have to do is to trust Christ, and trusting him, you will find him to be the way, from the beginning, even to the end.

Paid in Full

I must close by urging you to accept these words. "I am the way." Not merely, "I was the way for the thief on the cross," but "I am the way for you tonight." Not, "I will be the way when you feel your need more, and when you have worked yourself into a better state," but "Sinner, I am the way right now. I am the way for you, just as you are; I am the way to everything you lack."

We sometimes see railways approaching the city limits, but they do not bring the tracks right into the heart of town, you must take a cab or the bus to finish the journey. But this "way" runs right from the heart of humanity's hopelessness into the very center of glory, and there is no need to take anything to complete the trip.

You may remember what good Richard Weaver said when he spoke to us. He was illustrating the fact that Christ saves sinners and saves them right now. He told us a story of his friend in Dublin, Ireland, who bought him a first-class ticket for Liverpool, England, as he said, "All the way through." You will remember how he illustrated this by saying that, when he came to Christ, he put his trust in him, and had a first-class ticket to heaven all the way through. "I did not get out of the train to buy a new ticket," he said. "There was no fear that my ticket was only for halfway, because it was a ticket all the way through. I paid nothing," said Richard, "but that didn't matter. My ticket was enough. The guards came, and looked in, and said, 'Show your tickets, gentlemen.' They didn't say, 'Show yourselves,' but 'Show your tickets. They didn't come to the door, and say, 'Now, Mr. Weaver, you have no business in that first-class car. You are only a poor man. You must come out. You are not dressed well enough.' As soon as they saw my ticket, the ticket all the way through, that was enough. And so," said that man of God, "when the devil comes to me and says, 'Richard Weaver, how do you hope to get to heaven?' I show him the ticket. He says, 'Look at yourself.' 'No,' I say, 'that is just what I am not going to do. I look at my ticket.' My doubts and fears say, 'Look at what you are.' Ah! Never mind what I am. I look to what Christ gave me and what he bought and paid for himself, that ticket of faith that will surely carry me all the way through."

It is about arriving at your destination. The ticket, you see, will take you to the end. Christ is the way to the end. I want to show you, tonight, that Jesus is the way to heaven as well as to God himself. Christ has run the railroad right into heaven, but does it run from where I am? If it does not, if there is a space between me and the place where that railway stops, how am I to get there? I cannot take the taxicab of Morality, because the axle is broken. I will not get into the great bus of Ceremonies, because the driver has lost his license, and I am sure that will cause problems that will end the trip short. How am I to get there? I cannot get there at all unless the road comes right here to where I am. Well, praise God, it does come to just where you are tonight, sinner. There is nothing additional required of you. There is no preparing for Christ, no meeting Jesus Christ halfway, no cleaning yourselves up to let him give you the finishing touch, no mending your garments so he can add the crown. No. Just as you are, Christ says, "I am the way."

But you say, "Lord, what do you want me to do?" (NKJV) "Do?" says Jesus. "Do? Nothing except believe on me. Trust me. Trust me now." Did I hear someone up in the top gallery say, "When I get home tonight, I'll pray"? But this is not the gospel. The gospel is, trust Jesus Christ now. Christ is the way now; not only from your home to heaven, but from this place, from the very spot where you are now, to heaven.

My dear brothers and sisters, I emphasize again how much I detest from the bottom of my heart the new kind of legality that some ministers preach, who tell us we must not tell sinners to believe on Christ now, but that they must go through a process of conviction before believing. This is just another form of salvation by works. Conviction will follow if it has not already come. Instead, I lift up my Master's cross before the dying and the dead, before the blind, the ruined, and the filthy. Trust Jesus Christ and you are saved.

"But I have many sins." He had many drops of blood. "But I am a great sinner." He is a great Savior. "But I am so evil." His blood is so powerful that it can make you as pure as the new fallen snow. "But I am so old." Yes, but he can make you to be born again. "But I have rejected him so often." He will not reject you. "But I am the last person in the world who should be saved." Then that is where Christ begins; he always begins at the last man. "But I cannot believe that…" Cannot believe what? What did I ask you to believe? "I cannot believe…" I ask again, cannot believe what?

My Master is the Lord from heaven that cannot lie; and you tell me you cannot believe him! My Master never lied to angel or human. He cannot, because he is truth itself and this is what he says: He will save whoever will trust him. He will save you tonight. If you say you cannot believe him, you make God a liar, because you do not believe on his Son Jesus Christ. I caution you, by the coming day of judgment and the flaming sword of God, do not say that the God who made you will lie to you. Sinner, there will never be a spirit found in hell that can say, "I trusted Christ and was deceived. I rested on the cross and its rotten timbers creaked and failed me. I looked to the blood of Jesus and it could not cleanse me. I cried to heaven, but heaven would not hear. I took Jesus in my arms to be my Mediator and yet I was driven from the gate of mercy. There was no pity for me." Never. There shall never be such a case.

I almost said I wish to God I was not preaching to depraved people. Yet, to whom else should I preach? It brings me great sorrow to know that so many of you will turn on your heels and say, "There is nothing in it."

Who among you will look to Christ? Why, those whom God has chosen; those in whom the Spirit, as the result of divine election, will effectually work. These will be the real trophies of the Redeemer's work on the cross. You have all heard the gospel tonight. When the trumpet of judgment is ringing in every human ear, when this solid earth is shaking, when the heavens bow before the Lord and the light of the stars pale in his glorious light; when you and I meet face to face, I will bear this witness, that I plainly told you the way of salvation. In that last great day, I will be able to say about each one of you, "If you perish, your blood does not lie at my door."

Is there anyone here who still thinks they are shut out of heaven, that they cannot be saved? It is to you that I add this extra word, "Jesus is able to save to the uttermost those who draw near to God through him." You may be black with robbery, or red with blood, or stained up to your neck with lust, but Jesus is still able to save. Trust him. Trust him with all your heart and you will find that he will surely bring you to the place where he will look on you with delight, because he has washed you in his blood.

EARLY OR LATE

A Sermon Delivered on Sunday Morning, December 10, 1865
by C. H. Spurgeon at the Metropolitan Tabernacle, London

Matthew 20:1-16

1 [Jesus said to his disciples], "For the kingdom of heaven is like a master of a house who went out early in the morning to hire laborers for his vineyard. **2** After agreeing with the laborers for a denarius a day *(a day's wage for a laborer),* he sent them into his vineyard. *(Each person is called on to work for the Lord and will be richly rewarded for doing so. The pay agreed to was regarded as a fair wage. No one will ever have a reason to complain that he served God for nothing. Those who enter his service early in the morning of their lives are the happiest.)* **3** And going out about the third hour he saw others standing idle in the marketplace, **4** and to them he said, 'You go into the vineyard too, and whatever is right I will give you.' **5** So they went. *(We are good-for-nothing until we serve God. We may be very busy, but until we live for God we have accomplished nothing.)*

"Going out again about the sixth hour and the ninth hour, he did the same. *(The day was half gone, and then three-fourths of it, and yet this patient master continued hiring laborers. If half our life is gone, or even three-fourths of it, the Lord will still receive us. He does not hire people the way the world does. "For my thoughts are not your thoughts, neither are your ways my ways, declares the* LORD.*")* **6** And about the eleventh hour he went out and found others standing. And he said to them, 'Why do you stand here idle all day?' **7** They said to him, 'Because no one has hired us.' He said to them, 'You go into the vineyard too.' *(This showed that the laborers were not hired because the master needed them, but because he was a generous person. Otherwise, why would the master employ them just as the sun was setting? In the Lord's vineyard, it is grace alone that chooses, calls, hires, and pays the workers.)*

⁸ "And when evening came, the owner of the vineyard said to his foreman, 'Call the laborers and pay them their wages, beginning with the last, up to the first.' ⁹ And when those hired about the eleventh hour came, each of them received a denarius. *(However late in life a person may be converted, they will enjoy the same privileges and promises as others. Free grace gives freely and does not find fault.)* ¹⁰ Now when those hired first came, they thought they would receive more, but each of them also received a denarius. ¹¹ And on receiving it they grumbled at the master of the house, ¹² saying, 'These last worked only one hour, and you have made them equal to us who have borne the burden of the day and the scorching heat.' *(This ungenerous spirit will creep in even among the servants of God, but it deserves to be cast out with intense dislike. We should rejoice in the richness of divine love to elderly converts. It is very improper for a child of God to envy the spiritual privileges of someone else.)*

¹³ "But he replied to one of them, 'Friend, I am doing you no wrong. Did you not agree with me for a denarius? ¹⁴ Take what belongs to you and go. I choose to give to this last worker as I give to you. ¹⁵ Am I not allowed to do what I choose with what belongs to me? Or do you begrudge my generosity? *(The sovereignty of God is justified as much in the enjoyments and privileges of saints as in their election to eternal life. In making all of his people equally dear to his heart, equally safe in Christ, and equal in justification and adoption, the Lord shows his undoubted right to do as he wills with his own, as much as when he chooses a certain number of sinners, and allows others to continue in their sins.)* ¹⁶ So the last will be first, and the first last."

Many who begin in the Christian religion and show great promise often disappoint us, while others who seem hopeless bring forth good fruit. Many are called by the Gospel, but few are really elect of God. And from those who truly obey the call, only a very few become distinguished for the grace in their hearts. Fully dedicated people are rare even among the chosen.

Introduction

We have often mentioned how important it is to study the Scripture in its proper context. We have no right to tear passages of Scripture from their proper settings and make them mean what they were not intended to teach. Therefore I have given you the meaning, according to my ability, that I think our Lord intended in this parable. Jesus rebukes those who fall into a spirit of legalism and begin calculating what they think their reward in the kingdom should be. This legal spirit is entirely out of place. Our reward comes from grace, not as something that is owed us.

I think I may now dwell on one very distinct fact taught in this parable without violating the main lesson. It is not right to disregard the main teaching of the parable, but having now explained it and made it as clear as we can, we believe that we are now authorized to focus on one of the main things mentioned in it.

This morning I intend to call your attention to the fact that the laborers were hired at different times of the day and this clearly teaches that God sends his servants into his vineyard at different times and seasons. Some are called in their early youth while others are not led into the service of the Master until their long years have brought them almost to the evening of life.

However, I must ask you to remember that *they were all called.* The Savior mentions this to teach us that no one comes into the kingdom of heaven by their own initiative. There are no exceptions. Every laborer for Jesus has been called in one sense or another. They would not have come unless they were called. All Christians are called. If someone was already what they should be, there would be no reason to urge and invite them to come to the gospel of Christ. But since human nature is perverted, and people exchange bitter for sweet and sweet for bitter, darkness for light and light for darkness, an outward call is necessary. A person needs to be invited, persuaded and pleaded with. To use the strong words of the apostle Paul, we must "implore you on behalf of Christ, be reconciled to God." Indeed, we go even further and acknowledge that, even though some people come to the vineyard in a spirit of legalism through this common call of the gospel, yet no one comes to Christ in spirit and in truth without a further call; the effectual call of God's Holy Spirit.

The general call is given by the minister, it is all that he can give. If the preacher attempts to give the specific call, as some of my hyper-Calvinistic brothers do, by confining the gospel call to a certain type of person and assume that they are able to discover God's elect themselves, and attempt to focus God's universal call only to those who they believe are the elect; if the preacher acts like this, he makes a sorry mess of it, and usually fails completely to preach the gospel of good news to the children of men. But when a man is content to do what he actually can, that is, preach the commandment, "Believe in the Lord Jesus, and you will be saved," and that God "commands all people everywhere to repent," then the general call is accompanied by the Holy Spirit's particular and special call to the chosen of God. This secret call is given in such a way that all who hear it will offer themselves freely on the day of God's power, they will turn to the Lord with all their heart. How are we to understand our Lord's words, "many are called, but few are chosen" unless those who are chosen are called by the preaching of the Word?

There are two callings. One is a general call to all who hear about Jesus. Many who hear this general call make it clear that they are not chosen. The other call is personal and especially to the elect, because "those whom he predestined he also called." To return to our point; every laborer in the vineyard was called in some sense. There is not a single exception to this rule in the entire Christian Church. The doctrine of free will cannot show even one example to prove itself. There is not a sheep in all the flock that came back to the shepherd without being sought after. There is not a single piece of money that jumped back into the woman's purse, she had to sweep the house to find it. I will go even further and say there is not even a single prodigal son in the entire family of God who ever said, "I will arise and go to my Father," until the Father's grace afflicted the prodigal through a mighty famine and taught the miserable prodigal, as he fed the pigs and "was longing to be fed with the pods that the pigs ate, and no one gave him anything."

I want you to notice another fact before I come to our subject at hand. That is, *all those who are called are said to have been hired.* Of course, in a parable no word is to be interpreted by itself. We must give the meaning by how it was intended in the context. But still, I think we may say that there is a similarity between hiring a laborer and the commitment of a soul to Christ. After a man has been hired he has no right to serve another master, because he serves the master who hired him. When a soul is called by grace into the service of the Lord Jesus Christ, they cry, "Oh Lord, other lords have had control over me, but now I will serve only you." They pull off the yoke of sin, with its pleasure and tradition, and take on the yoke that their Master says is easy and bears the burden that Jesus tells us is light. A hired servant must not work for anyone else, because they work for their master. And a person who is called by grace does not live for any harmful objective or motive, but only for their Master.

Again, a hired servant does not work for themself. They are not their own master. "You are not your own, for you were bought with a price." From now on they call no man "Master" on earth and remembers that they now serve a Master who is in heaven. There is a serious contract between the hired person and their master, and the spiritual contract between the true believer and their Lord is even more important. We have devoted ourselves to his service, we have given up all liberty of self-will, and now his will is our will and his command our command. All of our powers and enthusiasm should be, and by God's grace we hope will be, obedient to him who has hired us to work in his vineyard.

Now the word "hired" was used to convey the idea of a reward. Our Lord told this parable in answer to Peter's question, "See, we have left everything and followed you. What then will we have?" Peter was thinking in a legalistic way. Jesus shows the folly of this way of thinking by showing that sovereign grace does as it wishes with its own. Yet even though believers are not hired in an evangelical sense, they do not serve God for nothing. They will not work without a reward. "The wages of sin is death, but the free gift of God is eternal life in Christ Jesus our Lord." We will have our reward for what we do for the Master. And although it is not wages in the sense of God being obligated to us for the work we do, I assure you there will not be a single true hearted worker for God who will not receive the most blessed wages of grace from their Master in that last great day.

And now to our point. The master calls these hired servants of his at different hours of the day and a different shade of grace stands out in each case. The varieties of our Lord's glorious compassion and lovingkindness are displayed in the different hours when the chosen ones are called.

Early In the Morning

Everyone is not called by grace at the same time. We see in this parable that some are called early in the morning. These are especially happy! The earliest age when a child may be called by grace would be difficult for us to positively identify, because children are not all of the same age mentally when they are of the same age physically. We dare not speculate or limit the Holy One of Israel about how early a child may be saved. As far as our own observation goes, grace works on some young children at the very dawn of moral consciousness. There are, no doubt, children so advanced in intellect and awareness that the Spirit sets them apart as early as two or three years of age. However, we have noticed that the Master usually intends to take such children home very soon.

There have been interesting biographies that prove holiness may bloom and ripen in the youngest heart. In the 17th century, the puritan James Janeway wrote *Token for Children or, Some Examples of Children, in Whom the Fear of God was Remarkably Budding Before They Died.* These stories illustrate Psalm 8:2 where David says, "Out of the mouth of babes and infants, you have established strength because of your foes, to still the enemy and the avenger." Little children that we might suppose could only have babbled about toys have been able to speak with apparent deep knowledge of spiritual and especially heavenly things. It is certain that some have performed their life's work for the Master in their mother's arms. They have spoken of the Savior in a way that has melted a mother's heart and pricked a father's conscience, and then they have been taken home. The ancient Greeks had a saying, "Whom the gods love die young," which meant the gods wanted them to be with them in the afterlife. It is no small privilege to be admitted into glory so soon. Only glimpsed on earth and then snatched away to heaven, too precious to be left below. Precious child, how dear you were to the good God who sent you here and then took you home! Fair rosebud! In the perfection of your young beauty, you have been taken to be worn by the Savior over his heart. How can we mourn your removal to the skies?

No bitter tears for you are shed,
  Blossom of being seen and gone!
With flowers alone we strew your bed,
  Oh Blessed departed one!
Whose all of life, a rosy ray,
  Blushed into dawn and passed away.

"Early in the morning would also include those whose lives have passed the first hour of the day, but who have not yet wasted the second hour of the morning. I am speaking of those hopeful boys and girls who perhaps would rather I call them youths or young people. They have outlived infancy and childhood and have reached their teenage years. They are in the heyday and robustness of youth. They are youngsters who are more at home in the playground than in the workplace. Satan tells them they are better off enjoying sports and shopping than being busy in the vineyard. But even among these—and we praise divine love for it—the master of the house hires laborers for his vineyard. It is worthwhile to warn some of our brothers and sisters who seem to be very doubtful about the conversion of young teenagers, to warn them of being so harsh and suspicious. We have noticed, and I think those who watched our membership carefully will also have noticed, that among all the slips and falls that have caused us sorrow, we have had very little sorrow caused from those who were added to us as boys and girls.

I, myself, have baptized into Jesus Christ very early in their boyhood those who are now preaching the gospel with power, to the delight of their hearers. And there are among us those who began to be joyful followers of the Lord Jesus Christ while they were still in school and are now serving this church as honored servants of God. Some of us have gained an understanding of the things of the kingdom from a very early age. The Bible has been our first textbook, the guidebook of our youth, and the joy of our earliest years. We thank God for the many Timothys who are among us and have followed the faith of their mothers and grandmothers. And we thank God too for the young Samuels who have been brought to the Lord's house from infancy, and began serving as priests to God in the early morning of life, and have served him with all their hearts. Happy are those who are called early in the morning! They have special reasons for blessing and praising God.

> Grace is a plant, wherever it grows,
>   Of pure and heavenly root;
> But fairest in the youngest shows,
>   And yields the sweetest fruit.

Let us spend a minute thinking about the happy condition of those who are saved in childhood. Early in the morning the dew still sparkles on the leaves, the pink blush of dawn fills the skies and reveals the opening beauty of the day. Those who do not rise early miss this wonder. There is a charm about early conversion that is impossible to describe, lovely in freshness, and shining with joy. In childhood we notice a natural simplicity and childlike confidence that is seen nowhere else. There may be less understanding, but there is more loving. There may be less thought process, but there is more of simply believing on the authority of the Bible. There may be less deep rootedness, but there is certainly more of fragrance, beauty, and green growth. If I must choose the part of the Christian life where there is the most joy, next to the Promised Land itself, I think I would prefer the area of Christian experience that is closest to the sunrise, that is sown with seeds of love, and cheered with the delightful music of the birds of hope.

Early in the morning, when we have just risen from sleep, work is easy. Our labor in the vineyard is a cheerful exercise rather than the exhausting labor of those who bear the burden and heat of the day. The young Christian is usually not subject to the harsh treatment, and cares, and troubles of the world that others are. He has nothing else to do but serve his God. He is free from the embarrassments that surround so many of us and keep us from doing good when we know we should. The child has nothing to think about except his or her Lord. There are books and homework, but they can have a zealous spirit in the midst of them. There are childhood friends to whom we may be of service and to God through them, in innocence and simplicity. If I could choose the best time to work for Jesus, give me the blessed morning hours, when my heart is lightest and the pure sunbeams of joy light my path; when my glowing heart has no lack of enthusiasm and my happy spirit is not burdened with care.

One would prefer early conversion because such people have not learned to stand around idle all day. If you have known someone, who has been standing around for hours with his hands in his pocket, talking with worthless fellows and so on, then you know he is not worth much at the eleventh hour, or even by the middle of the day, because he is in the habit of leaning against the walls and is not likely to take to work very eagerly. Begin early with your souls, break in the colts while they are young, and they are likely to accept the harness. There are no workers like those who began working while they were still children. What a promise of a long, productive day there is for young believers. The sun has just risen, and it must travel to its zenith and descend again. There is no time to spare, but there is plenty of time. If God brings a youngster to himself when there is still twelve hours left in the day—what may they not accomplish?

Early holiness may not be absolutely necessary for a grand and glorious life, but it is certainly a very great advantage. Giving those first days to Jesus will spare us many sad regrets, keep us from acquiring many evil habits, and equip us to achieve good success through the Holy Spirit's blessing. It is good to begin to fly while the wings are still strong. If we live in sin for a long time, our wings may be broken and then they will flap helplessly through the rest of our days, even when grace calls us to Jesus. Parents! Let it be your desire to have your children converted as children. And oh, may God put the desire into the hearts of some of you young people here this morning that, before you reach the age of twenty-one, before you are called adults, that you may be perfect men and women in Christ Jesus. May you become children of God while you are still children. May the Lord grant you to be like newborn infants who "long for the pure spiritual milk" and grow by it. Happy, happy, happy souls are those who the Master brings "early in the morning" by his distinguishing grace.

The Third Hour

The master of the house went out again "about the third hour." This may represent the beginning of adulthood. Suppose we think of the first hour as including people up to seven or eight years old; then the second hour runs from about then to twenty-one or thereabouts; and then we look at the third, fourth, and fifth hours as people in their twenties and early thirties. There are some who divine grace regenerates at the third hour. This is late! Twenty-one is seriously late, when you consider how much possible early joy is now lost forever, how many sins have now become habitual, and how many opportunities for usefulness have slipped away. A quarter of the day has flown away forever when we reach the third hour. The best quarter of the day, too, has gone and can never be recalled. The first meal of the day is over. Breakfast with Christ is no longer possible. It is a very precious meal when the Savior gives us the morning portion. The Israelites were supplied with sweet manna morning by morning, "but when the sun grew hot, it melted." Happy is the child who feeds on Jesus. Truly I remember when I was like Elijah sleeping under a broom tree and the angel said to him, "Arise and eat." The flavor of those delicious meals remains with me even now. The person of twenty-one has lost that first meal, breakfast is all over. Christ will say to him as he will to some others, "Come and dine," and that is precious; but the choicest meal is over, the first early enjoyment, the first early pleasure can never be known.

I have no doubt there are many here who think that being converted at twenty-one is quite soon enough. But why are twenty-one years given to Satan? Why is a fourth of a person's existence devoted to evil? Besides, it may not be a fourth, it may be one-half, and in many cases it is the entire life. The sun goes down before it is even noon and the idler has no hope of ever being a laborer in Christ's vineyard. Death comes when God wills and gives us no notice. It may cut down the flower before it has fully opened. It is "like grass that is renewed in the morning," but "in the evening it fades and withers." It is late. It is sadly late! It is very sad to have lost those bright days when the mind was less occupied with "the cares of the world," when it was most easily led to form godly habits. It is a sad thing to have learned so much about sin as one may have learned by twenty-one, a sad thing to have seen so much wickedness, to have treasured up in one's memory so much sinfulness.

In twenty years with God one might have become a good student in the kingdom, but after twenty years in the world one begins to be like a garment lying in the dye until it is stained through and through. It is late, but we thank God that it is not too late. Indeed, it is not too late even for the greatest accomplishments. Not only is this period of life not too late for salvation, but it is not too late to do much for Jesus Christ. Some of us had finished five years of Christian ministry by the time we were twenty-one and had been the means of bringing many souls to the cross of Christ. But if others are not led to Christ until they are twenty-one, there is still a good period of time remaining if God wills to spare our lives. The young man is now in all his strength and vitality and his heart is full of fire. He should have acquired a good amount of education and be prepared to acquire more.

He is just beginning the time when he should work. His plans for life are not settled yet; he is not married yet, and if he is there are probably no children around who have been injured by his bad example; he has an opportunity to raise a family in the fear of God. He may be beginning a business; if so, he has an opportunity to conduct that business in such a way that there may never need to be a time when he will have to change direction and chart another course. He may, if called by God's grace at twenty-one, begin an honorable career, in which there will be no need to alter his way or move the helm in order to enter straight to the harbor's mouth. He may steer on the sea and leave one shining wake that will reach in a direct line from the present moment straight to the lights of heaven and reach his port with his sail full and a priceless cargo on board to the praise of the glory of divine grace. It is late. In some ways it is very late. But, oh! it is not too late to serve the Master well, and to win a crown of great reward, the gift of divine love.

There is a great deal of work to do for those of us who are in this third, fourth, and fifth hour of the day. In fact, I suppose the Church must look to us for its most active work. By the ninth hour, a person often becomes more a receiver from the Church than a contributor to it as far as active involvement goes. To a great extent the Church's fresh blood, energy, warmth of heart, and willing action must come from young converts. Oh, you who are twenty-one, I wish you were all born from heaven! You young women, in your early beauty, may the Master in his infinite mercy bring you in! Oh, if you could know the sweetness of his love, you would not need persuading! If you could understand the joy of true religion, you would not need to be pleaded with! There is more holy cheerfulness enjoyed in secret with the Lord Jesus Christ, than in all the fun the world can provide. One ounce of Christ's love is better than a ton of the world's flatteries. The world offers colorful bubbles, nice to look at, but vanishing at a breath; but Christ gives real treasure that endures for eternity. The world offers fool's gold; it glitters, but it is not precious. There may be less glitter about the things of God, but there is solid joy and lasting pleasure known only to the children of Zion. May the Master come this morning to your hearts and use my simple words to call you at the third hour of the day into the vineyard.

The Sixth Hour

The Master's grace was not used up and therefore he went "out again about the sixth hour." We find him going to the marketplace at high noon. Half the day was over. Who is going to employ a man and give him a whole day's wages when twelve o'clock has come? He will not do too much if you give him a job at six, what will he do if you hire him at twelve? Half a day's work! That is a poor thing to seek or to offer. However, the Master seeks and accepts such laborers. He promises, "Whatever is right I will give you."

There are some who are found at the sixth hour and enter into the vineyard. They are saved by grace and begin their work for Jesus. This may represent the period that is supposed to be the prime of life, forty years old and older. This is sadly late, very sadly late. It is sadly late in a great many ways, not only because there is so little time left, but because so very much of the energy, and zeal, and strength, that should have been given to God, has been wasted; and has to some extent been used to fight against God.

Forty years of hardness of heart! That is a long time for God to be patient. Forty years of sin! That is a long time for the conscience to mourn over. Israel hardened their hearts in the wilderness for that long and God said, "Forty years I loathed that generation" and "Therefore I swore in my wrath, 'They shall not enter my rest.'" What a blessing for you who are forty and are still unconverted, that God has not sworn such a terrible oath about you, that his patience remains, that he continues to put up with you, that he still says to you, "Go, work my child—go work today in my vineyard."

It is sadly late, because it has become so much more natural for you to walk in the way of sin. You will have so much to contend with in the future as the result of your past. Turning the ship of the soul around is not such easy work as turning a ship by her helm. Only a divine hand can steer a soul on the course of grace. You will need much grace to conquer the depravity that has had forty years to take root. You have an occupant in your house that has possession of it and you will find that possession is nine-tenths of the law. It will be a hard eviction to bring about, so hard, in fact, that only "one stronger than he" can throw him out. To your dying day the memory of evil things that you heard during these forty years of being a non-Christian will stick with you. You will hear the echoes of an old song just when you are trying to pray. And some deed that you regret and mourn over will haunt you just when you are about to say, "Abba, Father," with a sincere heart. It is late. This sixth hour is very, very late. But it is not too late.

It is not too late for some of the richest enjoyments. You can still dine with Jesus. He can still reveal himself to you as he does not to the world. You can still have a great deal of time to serve him. It is not yet too late to be great among his servants. Take John Newton's life. He was called in the middle of the day, but John Newton left his mark in God's vineyard, a mark that will never be forgotten. I suppose Paul could not have been much younger when he was called by sovereign grace. In fact, most of the apostles were probably near forty when mercy met with them and they still did a glorious day's work. My brother, my sister, if you are saved by grace in midlife, you must work harder, you must ignore the time past when you served the will of the flesh, and now you must make "the best use of the time, because the days are evil." Why, someone converted at forty should move out at a double-quick time march to heaven. There should not be a moment lost. Work the engine at high pressure and give two strokes for every one that younger people and younger minds might. Seek for divine strength to do twice as much in the time remaining, since you have only half the time to do a life's work. I know you wish to win crowns for Christ, so then be up and doing, beloved. You are saved by grace and by grace alone. You want to honor Christ, because of his free love for you. Can you not attempt to honor him in the time remaining as others do during an entire lifetime? You may still serve the Master well with zeal, good judgment, carefulness and perfect consecration.

The Ninth Hour

The master of the house went out at the ninth hour. No one thinks of hiring day laborers at three o'clock in the afternoon. How can a day's work be done from three until six? This shows that the gospel is not about thinking enough good works and keeping the law will bring salvation. It must be all of grace or no one would think they could earn salvation with such a late start.

Well now, three o'clock in the afternoon, that is someone from sixty to seventy years old. The prime of life has gone. It is late. It is sadly late, very sadly late. It is late because all of the powers of the person are weak now. Their memory begins to fail. They think their judgment is better than ever, but that is probably only their own opinion. Most of their abilities lose their edge in old age. They have acquired experience, but still there is no fool like an old fool. Someone who has not been taught by divine grace learns very little of any lasting value by their experiences in life. Sixty thousand years would not make someone wise if grace did not teach them.

Now think about it. Is it not very late? Here is the man; if he is converted now, what is there left of him? He is just a candle end. He may give a little light, but it is almost like the stub of the candle burning in the socket. How have all of those sixty or seventy years been spent? Where have they been spent? Let us walk backward like Noah's two sons did when he was drunk and naked, and cover it all up; and oh, may almighty grace cover it too! The fact is terribly shocking—sixty, seventy years spent in the service of Satan! Oh what good the man might have done! What good he might have done if he had only served his God like he served the world! He has made a fortune, has he! How rich he might have been in faith by this time. He has built a house! Yes, but how he might have helped to build the Church. The man has been playing at casinos; he has been like boys by the seashore building castles of sand, that must all come down, and must come down very soon too, for I hear the surges of the dread tide of death, it is rolling in even now. Those teeth that have fallen out, arthritis and other pains, all show that this is not his rest. The tent that houses the soul is beginning to crumble around the man. The warning signs that remind him he must soon be gone are loud and clear. He must leave his wealth and possessions. If this is all he has in the end, it will turn out that he has done nothing. All he has done is piled up shadows and heaped together broken pottery. What might he have done if he had believed in Jesus? How much could he have accomplished for God and the souls of men?

What evil habits he has acquired! What can this man ever do? If he is saved, it will be as the apostle Paul says, "If anyone's work is burned up, he will suffer loss, though he himself will be saved, but only as through fire." He is called and he will enter heaven. But oh! how little can he do for the Master! And what strong evil habits he will have to wrestle against and what an inward conflict he will have even until he gets to heaven!

It is late. It is very late, but oh! blessed be God! it is not too late. We have had within these walls people who have long passed the prime of their days, who have come forward and said, "We will join you because the Lord is with you." We have heard their joyous story of how the old man has become a babe and how he who was gray with years has been born again into the kingdom of Christ. It is not too late. Did the devil say it was? The gate is closing. I can hear it grating on the hinges, but it is not shut! The sun is going down, but it is not yet lost beneath the horizon. If the Master calls you, run all the faster because he does. And when you are saved, serve him with all of your remaining strength and power, because you have so little time to glorify him here on earth. There is only a short time left to show your deep sense of indebtedness to his surpassing love.

The Eleventh Hour

The day is nearly over. The eleventh hour has come, five o'clock! The men have been looking at their watches to see if it will soon be six. They are itching to hear the clock strike. They hope the day's work will soon end. See; the Master goes out again to the marketplace. He sees those hulking fellows who are still loitering there and he selects some and asks them, "Why do you stand here idle all day? You go into the vineyard too and whatever is right I will give you" They come at the eleventh hour, probably half ashamed to begin so late. I imagine they were also half ashamed to have the others see them starting work so late. Still, they found work to do and there were generous laborers who looked over the tops of the vines and said to them, "Glad to see you, friends! Glad to see you, however late." There were a few, I dare say, among the laborers who would stop their work and begin to sing and praise God to think that their companions had been brought in at the eleventh hour; at least I know there are in this vineyard.

Now the eleventh hour must be looked on as any period of life that is past seventy years. I cannot tell how late it may extend. There is a verified case of a man converted to God at the age of a hundred and four. It was during the last revival in Ireland and he walked a great distance to make a confession of his faith in Jesus Christ. And I remember a case of a man converted in America by a sermon that he heard, I think, eighty-one years earlier. He was fifteen and living in England when he heard an evangelist who, at the end of his message, instead of pronouncing the blessing, said, "I cannot bless you. How can I bless those who do not love the Lord Jesus Christ? 'If anyone has no love for the Lord, let him be accursed.'" And eighty-one or more years later those striking words came to mind when he was living in America and God blessed them to his conversion.

There have been some who have been saved at the eleventh hour, at the very hour of death. It is not for me to know how many or how few, but there is one case we know of in the Bible. It was the dying thief on the cross. There is only one. However, God in his abundant mercy can do as he wishes to the praise of the glory of his grace. He can call his chosen even in the eleventh hour. It is very late. It is very, very, very late. It is sorrowfully late. It is mournfully late. But it is not too late! And if the Master calls you, come! If a hundred years of sin weigh you down so that your steps are painful and lame, come! If he calls you it is late, but not too late. Therefore, come. Have you thought of how the thief worked for his Lord? It was not a good place for working, hanging on a cross dying, just at the eleventh hour. But he did a great deal of work in those few minutes. Notice what he did. First, he confessed Christ. He acknowledged him as his Lord and confessed him before men. In the second place he justified Christ. "This man has done nothing wrong." In the next place he worshiped the Lord Jesus. He acknowledged him as a king with a kingdom. He even began to preach when he rebuked his fellow sinner and told him that he should not criticize one who was so unjustly condemned. He prayed what has become a very model prayer. "Jesus, remember me when you come into your kingdom."

At any rate, I wish I could say about myself what I can say about the thief. He did everything he could. I cannot say that of myself and I am afraid I cannot say it about any of you. I do not know anything the thief could have done on the cross that he did not do. As soon as he was called, he seems to have worked in the vineyard to the very best of his ability. So let me say to you my dear hearer, if you should be called at the eleventh hour, though you are quite old, yet for Jesus Christ's sake, out of great love for all the great things that he has done for you, go on in your life, and praise him with all of your might.

Special Grace

My time has gone. I wanted to point out to you the singular grace shown in every example in this parable. Those who are called in the early morning of life have great reason for admiring sovereign grace, because they are spared the sins and poor quality of life without God. However, I must be content with repeating the lines of 18th century Scottish churchman Ralph Erskine about those called in their early years.

> In heavenly choirs a question rose,
> That stirred up strife will never close;
> What rank of all the ransomed race,
> Owes highest praise to sovereign grace.
> Babes thither caught from womb and breast,
> Claimed right to sing above the rest;
> Because they found the happy shore,
> They never saw nor sought before.

What a special grace it is to be called when we were young! This is electing love. "When Israel was a child, I loved him, and out of Egypt I called my son." Some of us will need to sing a special song of thankfulness in time and in eternity, for the love that took us in our days of thoughtlessness and simplicity, and brought us into the family of God. It was not because we were better children than others, or because there was anything naturally good about us. We were just as willful, stubborn, high minded, proud, wayward, and disobedient as other children. And yet, mercy separated us from the rest. We will never stop adoring the sovereignty of grace.

Look at the grace that calls someone at the age of twenty, when the passions are hot, when there is strong temptation to plunge into evil and the so-called pleasures of life. To be delivered from the charms of sin will have our sweetest song. It is mighty grace that saves us when the world seems most attractive, that teaches us to consider "the reproach of Christ greater wealth than the treasures of Egypt."

To be called by the Lord at age forty, in the prime of life. This is a wonderful example of divine power, because worldliness is hard to overcome and worldliness is the sin of middle age. With a family around you, with the cares of your job, with the world eating into you like a disease, it is a wonder that God would visit you in his mercy, and regenerate your soul. You are a miracle of grace and you will feel it and praise God for it in time and eternity.

Sixty again. "Can the Ethiopian change his skin or the leopard his spots? Then also you can do good who are accustomed to do evil." And yet. And yet you have learned. You have had a blessed schoolmaster who lovingly taught you and you have learned to do good. Though your ship had begun to rot in the waters of the Black Sea of sin, you have a new owner and you will run up a new flag. You will sail around the Cape of Good Hope to the Islands of the Blessed, in the Land of the Hereafter.

But what shall I say about you who are called when you are senior citizens? Ah, you will have to love much, because you have had much forgiven. In your thankfulness, you should not be a whit behind those of us who are called in our early youth. We have much to bless God for and so do you. We are at one extreme and you at the other. We love much because we have been spared so much sinning. And you must love much because you have been delivered from so much sinning. Not to go through the fire is a reason for praising God. But to walk in the fiery furnace and not be burned, to be licked by the flame and to be delivered from its fierce fire, oh! how you should find words to express your gratitude! Whether called early or called late, called at midday or called at early noon, we have all been called by grace alone. Let us give all the credit to the Lord Jesus, and because of his mighty love, let us work for him with body, soul, and spirit; let us work until we can no longer work, and then praise him as we rest in glory.

I urge you, brothers and sisters, do not allow idleness to creep in. If you have tried to extend the Redeemer's kingdom, do it more. Give more, talk more about Christ, pray more, work more! People often advise me to do less. I cannot do less. Do less? Why, it would be better to rot altogether than live the inglorious life of doing less than our utmost for God. I am afraid none of us will kill ourselves by working too hard for Jesus. It would be such a blessed act of suicide to die by working too hard for the Lord, that if there is a sin that is excusable, it would certainly be that. I am not afraid that you are likely to commit such a crime. Work for the Master! Labor for the Master! We must spend and be spent, and wear ourselves out for him! "Make no provision for the flesh, to gratify its desires." And oh, how happy we will be, if we may have the privilege of finishing the work, and hearing him say, "Well done, good and faithful servant. Enter into the joy of your Master." May the Lord bless you for Christ's sake. Amen.

Portion of Scripture Read Before Sermon: Matthew 19:27-30 & Matthew 20:1-29, but Spurgeon's comments during that reading are not available. His comments on Matthew 20:1-16 (above) are taken from his work *The Interpreter.*

THE SHAMEFUL SUFFERER

A Sermon Delivered on Sunday Morning, January 30, 1859
by C. H. Spurgeon
at the Music Hall, Royal Surrey Gardens, London

Hebrews 12:2

Looking to Jesus, the founder and perfecter of our faith, who for the joy that was set before him endured the cross, despising the shame, and is seated at the right hand of the throne of God.

Introduction

Where can language be found to describe the matchless, unparalleled love of my Savior to the children of men? We sing with Charles Wesley, "Oh what shall I do, my Savior to praise?" We may find a great abundance of words and speak easily on any ordinary subject, but this subject goes beyond the ability of all words and eloquence. This is one of the unspeakable things. Unspeakable, because it surpasses thought and defies the power of words. How can we deal with that which is beyond our comprehension? I am aware that all I can say about the sufferings of Jesus this morning will be like a drop in the bucket. None of us know the half of the agony he endured; none of us have ever fully understood "the love of Christ that surpasses knowledge." Scientists have probed the earth to its center, plotted the path of planets, measured the skies, weighed the hills, even weighed the world itself; but this is one of those vast, boundless things, that surpasses the comprehension of all but God himself. Like the swallow that skims the water and does not dive into its depths, so all descriptions the preacher can give of the love of Christ only skims the surface. The immeasurable depths lie far beneath our ability to see them.

A poet put it this way:

O love, thou fathomless abyss!

The love of Christ is measureless and fathomless. None of us can completely understand it. In speaking on this topic today, we feel our own weakness, we cast ourselves on the strength of the Holy Spirit; but even then, we feel that we can never succeed in showing the depth of this subject. Before we can get a right idea of the love of Jesus, we must understand his previous glory in its majesty, and his becoming a man on the earth in all its depths of shame. Who can comprehend the majesty of Christ? When he was enthroned in the highest heavens he was, as the Nicene Creed says, "very God of very God." He was the Supreme Being. He made the heavens and all the angels. By his power he hung the earth on nothing, his own almighty arm held the planets and stars in place. He was always surrounded by the praises of angels, archangels, cherubim and seraphim, the full chorus of the Hallelujahs of the universe continually flowed at the foot of his throne. He reigned supreme above all his creatures. He was God over all and blessed forever. Who can measure his greatness? And yet this must be accomplished before we can begin to imagine that mighty descent he took when he came to earth to redeem our souls.

On the other hand, who can tell how far he lowered himself? To be a man was something, but to be a man of sorrows was far more. To bleed, and suffer and die; these are great things for him who was the Son of God; but to suffer such unparalleled agony as he did, to endure a death of shame as he did, to be deserted by his God when he was dying, this is a deeper condescending love than the most inspired mind can begin to understand and describe. And yet, we must first understand the infinite majesty and then the infinite shame before we can understand the love of Jesus Christ. The difference is literally from heaven to hell.

Shall we neglect this subject simply because we cannot fully understand it? Should we avoid it because we cannot measure its depths? No! Let us go to Calvary this morning and see this great sight. Jesus Christ, who for the joy that was set before him endured the cross, despising the shame.

I will try first, to show you the shameful sufferer. Second, we will talk about his glorious motive. And then in the third place, we will offer him to you as a worthy example to follow.

The Shameful Sufferer

Beloved, I wish to show you THE SHAMEFUL SUFFERER. The text speaks about shame and so before talking about suffering, I will attempt to say a word or two about shame.

There is perhaps nothing that people fear more than shame. We find that death itself has often been preferred to shame in the minds of men. Even the most wicked and hardhearted have dreaded the shame and contempt of their fellow creatures far more than any tortures to which they could have been exposed. In the book of Judges we read about Abimelech murdering his own brothers with no misgivings. But we find even this callous man overcome by shame, when "a certain woman threw an upper millstone on Abimelech's head and crushed his skull. Then he called quickly to the young man his armor-bearer and said to him, 'Draw your sword and kill me, lest they say of me, "A woman killed him."' and his young man thrust him through, and he died." Shame was too much for him. Abimelech would far rather commit suicide (for that is what it was) than suffer the shame of having it known he was slain by a woman. The same can be said for King Saul. Here was a man who was not ashamed of breaking his oath and hunting his own son-in-law like "a partridge in the mountains." Yet he fell on his own sword rather than having it be said that he fell at the hand of the Philistines. And the prophet Jeremiah tells us that King Zedekiah, who although he lived a reckless life, was afraid to fall into the hands of the Chaldeans, for fear that the Jews who had deserted over to them would mock him.

These examples are only a few of many. It is well known that criminals have often had a greater fear of public contempt than anything else. Nothing can break the human spirit like being subject to continual contempt, the clear and obvious contempt of peers. In fact, to go even further, shame is so frightening to people that it is one of the ingredients of hell itself. It is one of the bitterest drops in that awful cup of misery. The shame of everlasting contempt to which the will awake in the day of their resurrection; to be despised by men, despised by angels, despised by God, is one of the depths of hell. Shame is a terrible thing to endure. Many of the proudest natures have been brought down when faced with it. In the Savior's case, shame would be especially shameful. The nobler a person is, the more they sense the slightest contempt, the more intensely they feel it. An ordinary person might experience contempt without suffering, but someone who is used to being obeyed and who has always been honored would suffer bitterly. Despised monarchs and princes reduced to poverty are among the most miserable of men. But here was our glorious Redeemer, the second person in the Godhead, despised and spit on, and mocked. Imagine the shame his noble nature endured! Some birds of prey can be caged, but the eagle cannot bear to be tricked and blindfolded; he has a nobler spirit than that. The eye that has seen the sun cannot endure darkness without a tear. But Christ who was more than noble, beyond noble, beyond even royal ancestry, for him to be shamed, and mocked, must have been dreadful indeed.

Some people are of such a delicate, sensitive disposition that they feel things far more than others. Some of us are not so easily offended, or when we do perceive the affront, we are totally indifferent to it. But there are others of a loving and tender heart. They have wept for others' sorrows so much that their hearts have become tender and they feel the slightest brush of ingratitude from those they love. Words of swearing and criticism against them, from those for whom they are willing to suffer, would pierce their souls in the tenderest places. A man in armor could walk through thorns and briars without feeling, but a man who is naked feels the smallest of the thorns. Now in that sense Christ was a naked spirit, he had stripped himself of everything for humanity. Jesus said, "Foxes have holes, and birds of the air have nests, but the Son of Man has nowhere to lay his head." He stripped himself of everything that could make him callous, because he loved with all his soul. His strong passionate heart was focused on the welfare of the human race. He loved them "even to death." This was pain indeed; to be mocked by those for whom he died, to be spit on by the creatures he came to save, to come to his own, and find that his own did not receive him, but actually cast him out. Those of you with tender hearts that can weep for others' sorrows, and you that love with a love as strong as death, and with a jealousy as cruel as the grave, you can guess, but only you, what the Savior must have endured when everyone mocked, and scorned him, and no one pitied him or came along side to comfort.

To go back to the point where we started: Shame is especially repulsive to manhood and even more so to the unique and surpassing, noble, sensitive, and loving nature of Jesus Christ.

The Nature of Christ's Shame

Let us now behold the pitiful spectacle of Jesus put to shame. He was put to shame in three ways: by shameful accusation, shameful mockery, and shameful crucifixion.

Behold the Savior's shame in HIS SHAMEFUL ACCUSATION. He in whom there was no sin and who had done no wrong was charged with sin of the blackest kind. He was arraigned before the Sanhedrim on no less a charge than that of blasphemy. Could Jesus blaspheme? Could he who said, "My food is to do the will of him who sent me," blaspheme? Could he, who when in the depths of his agony, when "his sweat became like great drops of blood" and at last cried, "Father, not my will, but yours, be done," could he blaspheme? No. And it is just because the charge was so contrary to his character that he felt the accusation. If some of you here today were charged with blasphemy it would not startle you, because you have done it, and have done it so often you have almost forgotten that God abhors blasphemers, and that, "the Lord will not hold him guiltless who takes his name in vain."

But for one who loved as Jesus loved, and obeyed as he obeyed, for him to be charged with blasphemy, that accusation must have caused him severe pain. We are almost surprised that he did not draw back and fall to the ground like his betrayers did when they came with Judas to take him prisoner. An accusation like that might destroy an angel's spirit. Such slander might dry up the courage of a cherub. Do not marvel, then, that Jesus felt the shame of being accused of such a crime as this.

The high priest and Pharisees were not content with this. Having charged him with breaking the "First Table" of the ten commandments (that deals with our relationship with God), they then charged him with violating the second tablet (that deals with our relationship with our fellow men). They said he was guilty of rebelling against the government, that he was a traitor to the rule of Caesar, that he stirred up the people and declared that he was a king. Could Jesus commit treason? Could he who said, "My kingdom is not of this world. If my kingdom were of this world, my servants would have been fighting"? Could he who, when the people would have taken him by force to make him a king, withdrew to the wilderness and prayed, could he commit treason? Impossible! Did he not pay the tax in his poverty by sending Peter to the sea to find the shekel in the fish? Could he commit treason? He could not sin against Caesar, because he was Caesar's lord. He was the King of kings and Lord of lords. If he had chosen, he could have taken the purple robe from the shoulders of Caesar and with one word given Caesar over to be eaten by worms. Jesus commit treason? Far be it from Jesus, the gentle and mild, to stir up sedition or set man against man. No. He was a lover of his country and a lover of his race. He would never provoke a civil war. Yet this was the charge brought against him. Good citizens, and good Christians, what would you think if you were charged with such a crime? How would you feel if your own people were crying out against you and saying you were such a terrible criminal that you must be executed? Would that not embarrass and shame you? Your Master had to endure the charge of treason as well as blasphemy. He despised the shameful indictments and "he was numbered with the transgressors."

But next, Christ not only endured shameful accusation, he also endured *shameful mocking.* When Christ was taken away to Herod, "Herod with his soldiers treated him with contempt and mocked him." The original word for "contempt" means "nothing." Herod treated Christ like he was nothing. It is an amazing thing to find that a man should make nothing of the Son of God, who "is all in all." In Psalm 22, David spoke prophetically of the Christ saying, "I am a worm and not a man, scorned by mankind and despised by the people," but what a sin it was, and what a shame it was, when Herod made Christ nothing. Jesus could have withered Herod with one glance of his fire-darting eyes. Yet Herod may mock him, and Jesus will not speak, and soldiers may circle him, and mock his tender heart with their cruel jokes, but not a word has he to say, but "like a lamb before its shearer is silent, so he opens not his mouth."

Observe, from Christ being mocked in Herod's presence until Pilate "washed his hands before the crowd" and sent him on to his crucifixion, and then onward to his death, there were mockers of many kinds. In the first place, they mocked the Savior's person. One of those things about which we may say but little, but we should often think about, is the fact that our Savior was stripped in the presence crude of soldiers. All of the garments he had were removed. It is a shame even for us to speak about this that was done by our own flesh and blood to our Redeemer. The holy body that was the jewelry box of the precious gem of his soul was exposed to the shame and open contempt of vulgar-minded men who were utterly destitute of every particle of decency.

The person of Christ was stripped twice. For obvious reasons, our painters cover Christ on the cross, but there he hung, the naked Savior of a naked race. He who clothed the lilies had nothing with which to clothe himself. He who had clothed the earth with jewels and made robes of emeralds for it, did not have so much as a rag to conceal his nakedness from a staring, gazing, mocking, hardhearted crowd. He "made for Adam and for his wife garments of skins and clothed them" when they were naked in the garden; he took the loincloths they had sewn together from fig leaves to cover their nakedness and gave them something they could wear to protect themselves from the cold. But now they divide "his garments among them by casting lots" while he is exposed to the pitiless storm of contempt with nothing to cover his shame. They mocked his person. Jesus Christ declared himself to be the Son of God. They mocked his divine person as well as his human person. When he hung on the cross, they said, "If you are the Son of God, come down from the cross." "Let him come down now from the cross, and we will believe in him."

They often challenged him to prove his divinity by turning aside from the work he had come to do. They asked him to do the very thing that would have disproved his divinity, so they could, as they declared, acknowledge and confess that he was the Son of God. Can you think of it? Christ was mocked as man, we can picture him surrendering to this. But to be mocked as God! A challenge can be thrown to manhood and manhood would easily take it up and fight the duel. Christian manhood would allow the gauntlet to lie there, or trample it beneath its foot in contempt, bearing all things and enduring all things for Christ's sake. But can you imagine God being challenged by his creature, the eternal Jehovah provoked by the creature that his own hand had made, the Infinite despised by the finite; he who is "far above all rule and authority and power and dominion," by whom "all things hold together," laughed at, mocked, despised by the creature of an hour, who is "crushed like the moth"? This was extreme contempt, a contempt of his combined person, of his manhood and his divinity.

Next, notice they mock him in all his offices as well as his person. Christ is a king, and there was never before such a king. He is Israel's David; the hearts of whose people are united with him. He is Israel's Solomon; he will reign "from sea to sea, and from the River to the ends of the earth!" He was of a royal race. We have some on earth whom we call kings. The children of Nimrod are called kings, but they are not kings. They borrow their dignity from him who is the King of kings and the Lord of lords. But here was one of the true blood, one of the royal race, who had left his throne, and was mixed in with the common herd of mankind. What did his people do? Did they bring crowns with which to honor him? Did the nobility of the earth cast their robes beneath his feet as a carpet for his footsteps? See what they do! He is delivered up to rough and brutal soldiers. They find a mock throne for him, and having put him on it, they strip him of his own robes, they find some soldier's old cloak of scarlet or purple, and put it on him. They interlace thorns into a crown and put it on his head, a head that was adorned with stars from the beginning of time; and for a scepter they place a reed in his hand, a hand that will not resent an insult; and then, bowing the knee, they pay their fake homage before him, making him a mock king to be laughed at and ridiculed.

There is, perhaps, nothing so heartrending as royalty despised. You have read the story of an English king, who was taken out by his cruel enemies to a ditch. They seated him on an anthill, telling him that was his throne, and then they washed his face in the filthiest puddle they could find. With tears running down his cheeks, he said, "The day will come when I will once again bathe in clean water," though he was bitterly mistaken. But think of the King of kings and Lord of lords. For admiration he had the spittle of guilty mouths, for respect the striking of filthy hands, for praise the wit of brutal tongues! Was there ever shame like yours, oh King of kings? The emperor of all worlds was defied by soldiers and struck by their harsh hands. Oh earth! How could you tolerate this wickedness? Oh you heavens! Why did you not in anger crush the men who blasphemed your Maker? The king is mocked by his own subjects. Here was shame indeed.

We all know, too, that Jesus was a prophet. How did they mock him as a prophet? They blindfolded him; they shut out the light of heaven from his eyes, and they struck him and slapped him, and said, "Prophesy to us, you Christ! Who is it that struck you?" They demanded the prophet prophesy to those who taunted him, to tell them who it was that struck him. We love prophets; it is natural for humanity to love a prophet if we believe in him. We believe that Jesus was the first and the last of prophets. All others are sent by him. We bow before him in great admiration and adoration. We count it our highest honor to sit at his feet. Like Mary; we only wish we could have the comfort to wash his feet with our tears and wipe them with the hairs of our head. We feel, like John the Baptist, that we are not worthy to even untie the strap of his sandal. We cannot bear the spectacle of Jesus the prophet, blindfolded and repeatedly, violently struck with insults and blows.

They also mock his priesthood. Jesus Christ came into the world to be a priest, to offer sacrifice. These haters of the Lord must mock his priesthood too. Salvation was in the hands of the priests and now they say to him, "Let him save himself, if he is the Christ of God, his Chosen One!" Yes, he did save others and that is why he could not save himself. The scorn he received as our High Priest must remain a mystery to us, what unimaginable depths of shame they were. The Son of God, our great High Priest, the Passover Lamb, the altar, the priest, the sacrifice, the Lamb of God that takes away the sins of the world, is despised and mocked.

He was mocked, still more, in his sufferings. I cannot venture to describe the sufferings of our Savior under the lash of the scourge. St. Bernard, and many of the early fathers of the Church, give such a description of Christ's scourging, that I could not endure to tell it again. I do not know if they had enough data for what they say, but I do know, "he was wounded for our transgressions; he was crushed for our iniquities; upon him was the chastisement that brought us peace, and with his stripes we are healed." I know it must have been a terrible scourging, to be called wounding, crushing, chastisement, and stripes. And remember, every time the lash fell on his shoulders, the laugh of him who used the lash was included with the blow, and every time the blood poured out afresh, and the flesh was torn off his bones, there was a jest and a jeer, to make his pain more tragic and terrible.

And when he came to the cross, they nailed him on it, and continued to mock his sufferings! We are told that the high priests and the scribes stood by and watched him there. When they saw his head fall upon his breast, they would, no doubt, make some bitter remark about it. They may have said something like, "Ah, he will never lift his head again among the multitude." When they saw his hands bleeding they would say, "Ha, ha, these were the hands that touched the lepers and raised the dead, they will never do that again." And when they saw his feet, they would say, "Ah, those feet will never walk this land again, his journeys of mercy are finished." Then some coarse, some villainous, some brutal, perhaps some horrible joke would be made about every part of his loving character. They mocked him, and, at last, he called for drink, and they gave him vinegar; mocking his thirst, while they pretended to relieve it.

I have one more thing to notice and it is the worst of all. They mocked *his prayers*. Did you ever read in all the accounts of executions or murders that men ever mocked the prayers of their fellow creatures? I have read stories of some dastardly villains who were about to execute their enemies, and seeing their death approaching the victims have said, "give me a moment or two for prayer," and only in very rare cases has this been denied. I have never read of a case in which, when the prayer was spoken, it has been laughed at, and made the object of wisecracks. But here hangs the Savior, and every word he speaks becomes the subject of a pun or something to joke about. And when at the end he cries out the most electrifying death scream that ever shook earth and hell, "Eloi, Eloi, lema sabachthani?" even then they must twist it into a pun and say, "He is calling Elijah." "Let us see whether Elijah will come to take him down." He was mocked even in his prayer. Oh Jesus! Never was love like yours; never has there been patience that could be compared with what you endured when you "endured the cross, despising the shame."

I feel that in describing the ridicule the Savior experienced, I have not been able to fully communicate the shame through which he passed. I will attempt it again, in another moment, when I come to describe his *shameful death*, by taking the words that come before the ones on which I have been commenting. He endured the cross just as he despised the shame.

The cross! The cross! The word "cross" does not usually awaken thoughts of shame. There are other methods of capital punishment that appear to be more disgraceful than the cross. There is disgrace with the guillotine, and more dishonor to be hung on the gallows. But, remember, that although death by hanging is considered a death of shame, that shame is nothing compared with the shame of the cross, as it was understood in the days of Christ. We are told that crucifixion was a punishment reserved only for slaves, and, even then, the crime must be of the most horrendous kind. Only offenses like betraying a master, or plotting his death, or murdering him would have brought crucifixion, even on a slave. It was looked on as the most terrible and frightful of all punishments.

All the deaths in the world are preferable to crucifixion. They all have some slight lessening of the event, either their quickness or their glory. But this is the death of a villain, of a murderer, of an assassin; a death painfully extended, one that cannot be equaled in all the inventions of human cruelty, for suffering and humiliation. This is the death Christ endured! The cross in our day, I repeat, does not indicate shame. It has been the crest of many a king, the banner of many a conqueror. To some it is an object of adoration. The finest sculptures, the most wonderful paintings, have been dedicated to this subject. The cross in the form of jewelry has become popular and even respected. I believe we are unable, in this day, to fully understand the shame of the cross. But the Jew knew it. The Roman knew it. And Christ knew what a frightful thing, what a shameful thing it was to be put to death by crucifixion.

Remember too, that in the Savior's case, there were special aggravations of this shame. He had to carry his own cross. He was also crucified at the common place for executions. Calvary was a place that attracted crowds to watch people die. He was put to death at a time when Jerusalem was full of people. It was the feast of the Passover, when the crowd had greatly increased, and when representatives of all nations would be present to behold the spectacle. We read in the book of Acts that Parthians and Medes were there, as well as Elamites and residents of Mesopotamia in Greece, and perhaps far off Tarshish, and the islands of the sea. They were there to unite in this scoffing and to increase the shame. And he was crucified between two thieves, as if to teach that he was worse than they. Was ever shame like this?

Let me guide you to the cross. The cross, the cross! Tears begin to flow at the very thought of it. The rough wood is laid on the ground. Christ is flung on his back. Four soldiers grab his hands and feet. His blessed flesh is torn with the accursed nails. He begins to bleed. He is lifted into the air and the cross is dashed into the place prepared for it, every limb is dislocated, every bone put out of joint by the terrific jolt. He hangs there naked to his shame, gazed on by onlookers. The sun shines hot on him, fever begins to burn, the tongue is dried up and sticks to the roof of his mouth, he has nothing to relieve his thirst. His body is already weak through fasting. He has been brought near the brink of death by scourging in the hall of Pilate. Here he hangs, the tenderest part of his body, his hands and feet, are pierced, the most numerous and tender nerves fearfully ripped apart by the nails. The weight of his body drags the spikes up his foot, and when his knees are so weary that they cannot hold him, the iron begins to drag through his hands. It is a terrible, horrible spectacle.

But you have only seen the outward. There was an inward you cannot see. If you could see it, though your eyes were like the angels, you would be struck with eternal blindness. There was the soul. The soul dying. Can you guess the pain of a soul dying? A soul never died on earth yet. Hell is the place of dying souls, where they die the everlasting second death. There, within the ribs of Christ's body, hell itself was poured. Christ's soul was enduring war with all the powers of hell, a fight greatly inflamed in those powers because it was the last battle they would ever be able to fight with him. And worse, he had lost that which is the martyr's strength and shield; he had lost the presence of his God. God himself was striking him. "It was the will of the Lord to crush him; he has put him to grief; when his soul makes an offering for sin." God, in whose presence Christ had always been, hid his face from him. There was Jesus, forsaken by God and man, left to tread the winepress alone, more than that, to be trodden in the winepress, and clothed in a robe dipped in his own blood.

Was there ever grief like this? No love can picture it! No heart can imagine the suffering of Christ; and if it could, it could not give the thoughts words. The agonies of Jesus were like the furnace of Nebuchadnezzar, heated seven times hotter than any human had suffered before. Every vein in his body was a road for the hot feet of pain to travel; every nerve was a string on a harp of agony that vibrated with the harsh wail of hell. All the agonies that the damned can endure were forced into the soul of Christ. He was a target for the arrows of the Almighty, arrows dipped in the poison of our sin. All the waves of the Eternal dashed on this rock of our salvation. He must be bruised, trodden, crushed, destroyed. His soul must be "very sorrowful, even to death."

I must pause, I cannot describe it. I can tiptoe over it and you can too. "The rocks were split" when Jesus died. Our hearts must be made of harder marble than the rocks if they do not feel. The temple tore its gorgeous tapestry curtain; will you not also tear your hearts in mourning? The sun shed one big tear in its own burning eye, that quenched its light and caused "darkness over all the land;" will we not weep, we for whom the Savior died? Will we not feel an agony of heart because he endured this for us?

Pay close attention, my friends; all the shame that came on Christ, he despised. He counted it so light compared with the joy that was set before him, he is described as "despising the shame." As for his sufferings, he could not despise them. That word could not be used about the cross. The cross was too awful for even Christ to despise. He endured the cross. He could cast off the shame, but he must carry the cross, and to it he must be nailed. He "endured the cross, despising the shame."

Christ's Glorious Motive

"For the joy that was set before him." What was this joy? What was this GLORIOUS MOTIVE? The joy set before Jesus was primarily the joy of saving you and me. I know it was the joy of fulfilling his Father's will, of sitting down on his Father's throne, of being made "perfect through suffering;" but I also know that the grand, great motive of the Savior's suffering was the joy of saving us. Have you experienced the joy of doing good to others? If you have not I pity you, because of all the joys that God has left in this poor wilderness, this is one of the sweetest. Have you seen the hungry when they have lacked food for a long time? Have you seen them come to your house almost naked because they have sold their clothes to get money for food? Have you heard the woman's story of her husband's problems? Have you listened when you heard stories of prison, sickness, of cold, of hunger, of thirst? Have you never said, "I will clothe you, I will feed you." Have you never felt that divine joy when your money has been dedicated to the Lord by giving to the hungry? You may have whispered to yourself, "I should not feel self-righteous, but I do feel it is worth living to be able to feed the hungry and clothe the naked, and to do good to my poor suffering fellow creatures." This is the joy that Christ felt. It was the joy of feeding us with the bread of heaven, the joy of clothing poor, naked sinners in his own righteousness, the joy of finding mansions in heaven for homeless souls, of delivering us from the prison of hell, and giving us the eternal pleasures of heaven.

But why should Christ have compassion on us? Why should he choose to suffer for us? We never deserved anything from him. As a good old writer says, "When I look at the crucifixion of Christ, I remember that my sins put him to death. I do not see Pilate, but I see myself in Pilate's place, trading his life for honor from people, I do not hear the Jews crying out, but I hear my sins yelling, 'Crucify him, crucify him.' I do not see iron nails, but I see my own iniquities fastening him to the cross. I see no spear, but I see my unbelief piercing his poor wounded side,

"'For you, my sins, my cruel sins, his chief tormentors were;
Each of my sins became a nail, and unbelief the spear.'"

In the opinion of the Roman Catholic Church, the soldier who pierced Christ's side was later converted and became a follower of Jesus. I do not know if that is true, but, spiritually speaking, it is. I know we have pierced the Savior. I know we have crucified him. And yet, strange to say, the blood we caused to flow from those holy veins has washed us from our sins and "has blessed us in the Beloved." Can you understand this? Here is humanity mocking the Savior, parading him through the streets, nailing him to a cross, and then sitting down to mock his agonies. And yet what is there in the heart of Jesus? Only love, only love for them! He is weeping as they call for his crucifixion, he is weeping when they nail him to the cross. Yes, he is weeping because he felt the suffering, but much more because he could not bear the thought that men whom he loved could nail him to the tree.

"That was the most unkindest cut of all." You remember Shakespeare's *Julius Caesar*, when his friend Brutus struck him. "For when the noble Caesar saw him stab, ingratitude, more strong that traitors' arms, quite vanquished him. Then burst his mighty heart." Jesus had to endure the stab in his inmost being, and know that his elect did it, that his redeemed did it, that his own church was his murderer, that his own people nailed him to the tree. Can you think, beloved, how strong the love must have been that made him submit to even this?

Picture yourself today, going home from this meeting. You have an enemy who has been your enemy all his life long. His father was your enemy and he is also your enemy. There is never a day that passes but you try to win his friendship; but he spits on your kindness and curses your name. He injures your friends, there is not a stone he leaves unturned to do you damage. As you are going home today, you see a house on fire. The flames are raging and the smoke is rising in one black column to heaven. Crowds gather in the street, you are told there is a man on the second floor who will be burned to death. No one can save him. You say, "Why that is my enemy's house." You see him at the window. It is your own enemy; the very man, he is about to be consumed by the flames. Full of lovingkindness, you say, "I will save that man if I can." He sees you approach the house; he puts his head out the window and curses you. "An everlasting curse on you!" he says. "I would rather perish than have you save me." Do you imagine yourself then, dashing through the smoke, and climbing the blazing staircase to save him? Can you picture him, when you get near him, struggling with you and trying to roll you into the flames? Can you believe that your love for him would be so strong that you would rather die in the flames than leave him to be burned to death?

You say, "I could not do it; it is beyond human ability to do it." But Jesus did it! We hated him, we despised him. When he came to save us, we rejected him. When his Holy Spirit comes into our hearts to struggle with us, we resist him; but he will save us. He braved the fire so he could rescue us from eternal burning. The joy of Jesus was the joy of saving sinners. The great and glorious motive for Christ in enduring all this was to save us.

Imitate Christ

In closing, give me just a moment to hold the Savior up for OUR IMITATION. I am speaking now to Christians, to those who have tasted and handled the good word of life. Christian men! If Christ endured all this, merely for the joy of saving you, will you be ashamed of enduring anything for Christ?

> "If on my face for thy dear name, shame and reproach shall be,
> I'll hail reproach, and welcome shame, my Lord, I'll die for thee."

I am not surprised that the martyrs died for a Christ like this! When the love of Christ "has been poured into our hearts," we feel that if the stake were here we would stand firmly in the fire to suffer for him who died for us. I know our poor unbelieving hearts would soon begin to cower at the crackling wood and furious heat. But surely this love would overcome all our unbelief. Are there any of you who feel that if you follow Christ you would be the loser, you would lose your position at work, or lose your reputation? Will you be laughed at if you leave the world and follow Jesus? Will you turn back because of these little things when he would not turn back? The world mocked him right up to the time he said, "It is finished." By the grace of God, let every Christian lift his hands to the Most High God, to the maker of heaven and earth, and let him say within himself,

> "Now for the love I bear his name, what was my gain I count my loss,
> I pour contempt on all my shame, and nail my glory to his cross."

"For to me to live is Christ, and to die is gain." In living I will be his. In dying I will be his. I will live to his honor, serve him totally (if he will help me), and if need be, I will die for his name's sake.

Compel People to Come In

A Sermon Delivered on Sunday Morning, December 5, 1858
by C. H. Spurgeon
at the Music Hall, Royal Surrey Gardens, London

Luke 14:16-18b; 21-23

Jesus said, "A man once gave a great banquet and invited many. And at the time for the banquet he sent his servant to say to those who had been invited, 'Come, for everything is now ready.' But they all alike began to make excuses. So the servant came and reported these things to his master. Then the master of the house became angry and said to his servant, 'Go out quickly to the streets and lanes of the city, and bring in the poor and crippled and blind and lame.' And the servant said, 'Sir, what you commanded has been done, and still there is room.' And the master said to the servant, 'Go out to the highways and hedges and **compel people to come in**, that my house may be filled.'"

Compel People to Come In

I feel in such a hurry to obey this commandment this morning that I cannot wait for an introduction. I must immediately begin my work of compelling people who are now lingering in the highways and hedges to come in.

Listen. You who are strangers to the truth as it is in Jesus, hear the message I have been told to bring you. You have fallen, fallen in your father Adam. You have also fallen yourselves by your daily sin and constant wrongdoing. You have provoked the Most High to anger, and as surely as you have sinned, God must punish you if you persist in your sin, because the Lord is a God of justice and will not spare the guilty.

But have you not heard, has it not been told you many times that God, in his infinite mercy, has devised a way where, without damage to his honor, he can have mercy on you who are guilty and undeserving? I am speaking to you today. My words are to you. Jesus Christ, God the Son, has descended from heaven, and was made in the likeness of sinful flesh. He was fathered by the Holy Spirit and born of the Virgin Mary. He lived a life of perfect holiness in this world, and suffered deeply until at last he gave himself up to die for our sins, "the righteous for the unrighteous, that he might bring us to God." I now declare that plan of salvation to you: "Believe in the Lord Jesus, and you will be saved." To you who have violated all God's laws, and sneered at his mercy, and dared his vengeance, this mercy is proclaimed to you: "Believe in the Lord Jesus, and you will be saved." "The saying is trustworthy and deserving of full acceptance, that Christ Jesus came into the world to save sinners;" whoever comes to him he "will never cast out." Jesus "is able to save to the uttermost those who draw near to God through him, since he always lives to make intercession for them."

He gives this to you, and all God asks of you is that you will simply look at his bleeding dying son and trust your souls to the hands of him whose name alone can save you from death and hell. Is it not remarkable that the proclamation of this gospel is not received favorably by everyone? One would think that whenever this was preached, "That whoever believes in him may have eternal life," every person hearing would cast all their "sins into the depths of the sea," take hold of Jesus Christ, and look only to his cross. But sadly, the desperate evil of our nature, the destructive depravity of our character, makes this message despised. The invitation to the gospel feast is rejected, because many of you are enemies of God. Enemies by your wicked works and for refusing the God who preaches Christ through me to you today; enemies to the God who sent his Son to give his life a ransom for many. It is strange that it should be so, and yet it is a fact. That is why the command is needed, "Compel people to come in."

Children of God, you who have believed, I will have little or nothing to say to you this morning. I am going straight to my business; I am going after those who will not come, those who are in the highways and hedges, and God going with me, it is now my duty to carry out this command, "Compel people to come in."

Where Are You?

First, I must *find you,* and then I will go to work to *compel you to come in.*

I must *find you* before I can compel you. If you read the first part of our passage, you will find an expansion of this command:" Go out quickly to the streets and lanes of the city, and bring in the poor and crippled and blind and lame;" and then, "Go out to the highways," bring in the street people and the robbers, and then, the "hedges," bring in those who have no place to sleep, and are lying under the hedges to rest, bring them in too, and "compel them to come in." I see, this morning, you who are *poor*. I am to compel *you* to come in. You are poor financially, but this is not a roadblock to the kingdom of heaven. God does not withhold his grace from the person that shivers in rags and is without food. In fact, if God makes any distinction at all, it is on your side and for your benefit. It is to you that this salvation of God has been sent; "The poor have good news preached to them."

But I must speak especially to you who are *poor spiritually*. You have no faith, you have no virtue, you have no good work, you have no grace. And what is even greater poverty, you have no hope. Be glad, my Master has sent *you* a gracious invitation. Come, you are welcome to the wedding feast of his love. "Let the one who desires take the water of life without price." Come, I must bring you. Though you have nothing but rags to wear, though your own righteousness is filthy and patched, I must stop you, and invite you, and even compel you to come in if necessary.

I look again. I see that you are not only poor, but *crippled.* There was a time when you thought you could work out your own salvation without God's help, when you could perform good works, attend to ceremonies, and get to heaven on your own. The sword of the law has cut off your hands. You can no longer work for your salvation. You say, with bitter sorrow,

> "The best performance of my hands,
> Dares not appear before your throne."

You have now lost all power to obey the law. You feel that when you "want to do right, evil lies close at hand." You are crippled. You have given up all hope at attempting to save yourself, because you are crippled and your arms are gone. But you are worse off than that. If you could not work your way to heaven, you once thought you could walk your way there along the road by faith. But you are disabled in the feet as well as in the hands. You feel that you cannot believe, that you cannot repent, that you cannot obey the requirements of the gospel. You feel that you are entirely done for, powerless in every way to do anything that can be pleasing to God. In fact, you are crying out,

> "Oh, could I but believe,
> Then all would easy be,
> I would, but cannot, Lord relieve,
> My help must come from thee."

I am sent to you also. I am to lift up the bloodstained banner of the cross before *you*. I am to preach this gospel to you. "Everyone who calls on the name of the Lord will be saved." It is to you I cry, "Let the one who desires take the water of life without price."

There is still another group. You who are *lame*; you who are limping between two opinions. Sometimes you are serious about your soul, other times the merriment of the world calls you away. What little progress you do make in religion is only a limp. You have a little strength, but it is so little that your progress is slow and painful. My limping friend, this word of salvation is sent to you too. Though you limp between two opinions, the Master sends me to you with this message: "How long will you go limping between two different opinions? If the Lord is God, follow him, but if Baal, then follow him." Consider your ways. "Set you house in order, for you shall die, you shall not recover." "Because I will do this to you, prepare to meet your God." Limp no longer. Decide for God and his truth.

There is one other type of person mentioned, *the blind*. You cannot see yourselves. You think you are good when you are full of evil. You put bitter for sweet and sweet for bitter, darkness for light and light for darkness. I am sent to you also. You cannot see your lost condition. You do not believe that sin is really as bad as it is. You refuse to accept that God is a just and righteous God. I am sent to you who cannot see the Savior, that see nothing desirable in him. You see no excellence in virtue, no good in religion, no happiness in serving God, no delight in being his children.

For that matter, to who am I not sent? My text not only describes each individual, but goes on to make a general sweep and says, "Go out to the highways and hedges." This includes all classes of men and women; the rich man driving along, the woman struggling to survive, the thief robbing the traveler. All these are in the highway and they are all to be compelled to come in. There, over there in the hedges, there are some poor souls whose shelters of lies have been swept away, who are looking for some little place for their weary heads. We are sent to you this morning. The command is universal. "Compel people to come in."

We have described the people. Let us pause to look at the virtually impossible task that I have been given. Melanchthon, the German reformer who succeeded Martin Luther as the leader of the German Reformation Movement in the 16th century, said, "Old Adam was too strong for young Melanchthon." Trying to lead a sinner to the cross of Christ can be compared to a little child trying to compel a Samson. And yet my Master sends me on my errand. I see before me a great mountain of human depravity and cold indifference. But by faith I cry, "Who are you, O great mountain? Before Zerubbabel you shall become a plain." Does my Master say, "Compel people to come in"? Then, though the sinner is like Samson and I like a child, I shall lead him with a thread. If God says do it, if I attempt it in faith it shall be done. If I seek, with a groaning, struggling, weeping heart, to compel sinners to come to Christ today, then the sweet urging of the Holy Spirit will go with every word, and some will indeed be compelled to come in.

On to the Work

And now to the work, directly to the work. Men and women! You who are unconverted, unregenerate, at war with God; I AM TO COMPEL YOU TO COME IN. Allow me, first, to confront you in the highways of sin and again tell you what my errand is. The King of heaven sends a gracious invitation to you this morning. He says, "As I live, declares the Lord God, I have no pleasure in the death of the wicked, but that the wicked turn from his way and live." "Come now, let us reason together, says the Lord. Though your sins are like scarlet, they shall be as white as snow." Dear friend, it makes my heart rejoice to think I have such good news to tell you. But I must admit, my soul is heavy because I see you do not think it is good news, and turn away from it, and pay no attention to it. Allow me to tell you what the King has done for you. He knew your guilt, he saw that you would ruin yourself. He knew that his justice would demand your blood. And so, to overcome this difficulty, that his justice would be satisfied, and that you might be saved, Jesus Christ has died.

Will you think about this for just a moment? You see Jesus there on his knees in the garden of Gethsemane, sweating drops of blood. Then you see that sufferer in misery, tied to a pillar and whipped with terrible scourges until the shoulder bones are like white islands in a sea of blood. And then this same man is hanging on the cross with his hands outstretched and his feet nailed tight. He is dying, groaning, bleeding. Do you hear him cry, "It is finished"? Jesus Christ of Nazareth has done all this so that God can be consistent with his justice and still pardon sin. The message to you this morning is: "Believe in the Lord Jesus, and you will be saved." Trust him. Give up your works and your ways. Set your heart on Jesus alone, this man who gave himself for sinners.

Well brothers and sisters, I have delivered the message. How do you respond? Do you turn away? Do you tell me it is nothing to you; that you cannot listen to it; that perhaps you will listen to me some other time, and that you have other more important things to do right now? Stop brother! Stop sister! I was not instructed to merely tell you and then go about my business. No; I am told to compel you to come in. Before I go any further, let me assure you that I am in earnest; my desire is that you would comply with this command of God. You may despise your own salvation, but I do not despise it. You may go away and forget what you are hearing, but please remember that the things I am now saying cost me many a groan before I came here to say them. My inmost soul is speaking to you when I plead with you to consider my Master's message. He commands you to believe in him who lived, was dead, and is alive forevermore.

Do you reject my message? Do you still refuse to accept it? Then I must change my tone a minute. I will not merely tell you the message and eagerly and sincerely invite you to accept it. I will go further. Sinner, in God's name I *command* you to repent and believe. Do you ask me where I get my authority to command you to believe? I am an ambassador of heaven. My commission to preach the gospel is from God. I know this in my heart, and there are believers sitting and standing in this hall this morning, who were converted under my ministry, who can confirm my calling. Therefore, as the everlasting God has given me a commission to preach his gospel, I command you to believe in the Lord Jesus Christ. I do not do this on my own authority, but on the authority of him who said, "Go into all the world and proclaim the gospel to the whole creation;" after which he added this serious warning, "Whoever believes and is baptized will be saved, but whoever does not believe will be condemned." If you reject my message, remember this, "Anyone who has set aside the law of Moses dies without mercy on the evidence of two or three witnesses. How much worse punishment, do you think, will be deserved by the one who has spurned the Son of God?" An ambassador is not to stand below the person with whom he deals. He stands higher. If the minister takes his proper place, he sees himself as representing the all-powerful God and commissioned by him. He is to speak with that authority and "compel people to come in," "to reprove, rebuke, and exhort, with complete patience."

Do you turn away and say you refuse to be commanded? Then I will change my tune again. If one way does not work, then all other means will be tried. Brothers and sisters, I come to you in plain words and *urge* you to flee to Christ. Do you know what a loving Christ he is? Let me speak from my heart and tell you what I know about him. I, too, once despised him. He knocked at the door of my heart and I refused to open it. He came to me, times without number, morning by morning, and night by night. He troubled my conscience and spoke to me by his Spirit, until at last, the thunders of the law overcame my conscience to the point I thought that Christ was cruel and unkind. I can never forgive myself that I thought so badly about him. When I did go to him I found a loving reception. I thought he would strike me, but his hand was not clenched in anger but opened wide in mercy. I thought his eyes would surely shoot out lightning flashes of his anger on me. Instead, they were full of tears. He embraced me and kissed me. He took off my rags and dressed me with his righteousness. He made my soul sing for joy. There was music and dancing in my heart and in his church, because the son he lost was found, and he who was dead is alive.

So I urge you, look to Jesus Christ and be happy. You will never regret it. On my Master's honor, I promise you will never regret coming to Christ. You will have no desire to go back to your condemned state. You will go out of Egypt and into the promised land flowing with milk and honey. You will find the trials of the Christian life heavy, but you will find grace will make them light. "Taste and see that the Lord is good!" A child of God has joys and delights. I am not afraid to promise you that God is not only good, but also better than human lips can ever describe.

I do not know what arguments will persuade you. I appeal to your own self-interests. Oh my friend, would it not be better for you to be at peace with the God of heaven, than to be his enemy? What do you gain by opposing God? Are you happier for being his enemy? Answer—have you found delights in that cup of pleasure seeking? Answer—have you found peace wearing yourself out with your so-called good works? You who seek to go about establishing your own righteousness, let your conscience speak, be honest; have you found happiness on that path?

My friend, "Why do you spend your money for that which is not bread, and your labor for that which does not satisfy? Listen diligently to me, and eat what is good, and delight yourselves in rich food." I appeal to you by everything that is sacred and serious, everything that is important and eternal, flee for your lives. Do not look back, do not be like Lot's wife. Do not wait until you can prove what I say to your own satisfaction. The blood of Jesus Christ cleanses us from all sin, flee to Jesus and his life giving blood.

Are you still cold and indifferent? Will not the blind man allow me to lead him to the feast? Will not my lame brother put his hand on my shoulder and permit me to assist him to the banquet? Will not the poor man allow me to walk side-by-side with him? Must I use some stronger words? Must I use some other means to compel you to come in? Sinners, I am determined to accomplish at least one thing this morning; if you refuse to be saved you will be without excuse. You, from the senior citizen down to the tender age of childhood, if you will not lay hold on Christ today, your blood will be on your own head. If there is any power in man to bring a fellow human (as there is when that man is helped by the Holy Spirit) that power will be used this morning, God helping me. I refuse to be put off by your rejections; if my trying to persuade you fails, I must try something else.

My friends, I *plead* with you. I beg you to stop and consider. Do you know what it is you are rejecting this morning? You are rejecting Christ, your only Savior. "No one can lay a foundation other than…Jesus Christ." "There is no other name under heaven given among men by which we must be saved." I cannot bear that you should do this, because I remember what you are forgetting. The day is coming when you will want a Savior. It is not long before this life will draw to a close. Your strength will begin to decline, your pulse will weaken, your strength will depart, and you and the grim monster, death, must face each other. What will you do without a Savior when the swelling river overtakes you? Deathbeds are cold and hard without the Lord Jesus Christ. Death is an awful thing. Even the person with the best hope, and the most triumphant faith, finds that death is not a thing to laugh at. It is a terrible thing to pass from the seen to the unseen, from the mortal to the immortal, from time to eternity. You will find it hard to go through the iron gates of death without the sweet wings of angels to escort you to the gateways of the skies. It will be a hard thing to die without Christ. I cannot help thinking about you. I see you this morning, committing eternal suicide. I picture myself standing at your deathbed, hearing your cries, and knowing that you are dying without hope. I cannot bear that. I think I am standing by your coffin now, looking into your clay-cold face, and saying, "This person despised Christ and neglected such a great salvation." I think what bitter tears I will weep, if I think I have been unfaithful to you, and how those eyes, closed in death, will seem to rebuke me and say, "Minister, I attended the Music Hall, but you were not in earnest with me. You amused me, you preached to me, but you did not plead with me. You did not know what Paul meant when he said, 'We implore you on behalf of Christ, be reconciled to God.'"

I beg you; let this message enter your heart for another reason. I picture myself standing in God's courtroom. As the Lord lives, the day of judgment is coming. Do you believe that? You are not an infidel; your conscience would not permit you to doubt the Bible. You may have pretended to doubt, but you cannot. You feel there must be a day when God will judge the world in righteousness. I see you standing in the middle of that vast multitude. The eye of God is fixed on you. It seems to you that the Judge of all the earth is not looking anywhere else, but only on you. He summons you before him. He reads your sins, and he cries, "Depart from me, you cursed, into the eternal fire!" I cannot bear to think of you in that position. It seems as if every hair on my head must stand on end to think of my hearers being damned. Will you picture yourself in that position? The word has gone forth, "Depart, you cursed." Do you see the pit of hell as it opens to swallow you up? Do you listen to the shrieks and yells of those who have gone to the eternal lake of torment before you? It is a terrible scene. I join the inspired prophet, Isaiah, in saying, "Who among us can dwell with the consuming fire? Who among us can dwell with everlasting burnings?"

Oh my brother, my sister! I cannot let you disregard true religion like this; not as I think of what comes after death. I would be lacking all humanity if I should see someone about to poison himself and not knock the glass out of his hand; or if I saw someone else about to jump off a high bridge, and not attempt to help prevent them from doing so. I would be worse than a demon if I did not now, with all love, and kindness, and earnestness, beg you to "take hold of eternal life," "do not labor for the food that perishes, but for the food that endures to eternal life."

Some hyper-Calvinist would tell me I am wrong for talking to you like this. I cannot help it. I must do it. I must stand before my Judge as you must. I feel that I will not have fulfilled my ministry unless I plead with you with many tears to look to Jesus Christ and receive his glorious salvation. Do you say this does not help? Are all our appeals lost on you? Do you turn a deaf ear? Then I will try a different way to win you over.

My friend, sinner, I have pleaded with you as a man pleads with his friend. I could not speak more earnestly with you this morning if I were pleading for my *own* life. I feel earnest about my own soul, but not one bit more than I do about the souls of my congregation this morning. Therefore, if nothing I have said has worked, I must use something else. I must *warn* you. You will not always have warnings like these. A day is coming when the voice of every gospel minister will be hushed. At least for you it will be silenced, because your ear will be cold in death. There will be no more threatening, because the fulfillment of the threatening will be before you. There will be no promise, no proclamations of pardon, no mercy, no talk of peace giving blood. You will be where days of rest are swallowed up in everlasting nights of misery, where the preaching of the gospel is forbidden, because it would achieve nothing.

As an ambassador of Christ it is my duty to command you to listen to this voice that is now speaking to your conscience. If you refuse, God will speak to you in his anger, and say to you in his hot displeasure, "I have called and you refused to listen, have stretched out my hand and no one has heeded. Because you have ignored all my counsel and would have none of my reproof, I also will laugh at your calamity; I will mock when terror strikes you." Sinner, I threaten you again. Remember, you have only a short time to hear these warnings. You imagine your life will be long, but do you know how short it is? Have you ever thought about how frail you are? Have you ever seen a body examined by a pathologist? Have you ever seen such a marvelous thing as the human body?

> "Strange, a harp of a thousand strings,
>   Should keep in tune so long."

Let just one of those cords be twisted, let only a mouthful of food go down the wrong pipe, and you may die. The slightest chance, as we call it, may send you to a swift death, when God wills it. Strong men have been killed by the smallest and slightest accident and so may you. In the chapel, during a church service, men have dropped dead. How often do we hear of people falling in our streets from a sudden stroke or heart attack; rolling out of time and into eternity? Are you quite certain that heart of yours is completely sound? Is the blood circulating as it should? Are you absolutely certain? And if it is now, for how long? Christmas is less than three weeks away. Perhaps some of you here today will never see it. Perhaps the official order has already been given, "Set your house in order, for you shall die, you shall not recover." Out of this vast congregation, I might predict with accuracy how many will be dead in a year; it is certain that all of us will never meet together again in any one gathering. Some out of this vast crowd, perhaps some two or three, will depart before the new year is ushered in. I remind you, then, my friends, that either the gate of salvation may be shut, or you may be out of reach of that gate of mercy.

Come, then, let the power of these threats win you over. I do not threaten to alarm you without cause. I hope that a brother's threatening may drive you to the place where God has prepared the feast of the gospel. Must I hopelessly turn away? Have I exhausted everything I can say? No! I will come to you once more. Tell me what it is that keeps you from Christ. I hear someone say, "Oh, Pastor, it is because I feel too guilty." That cannot be, my friend, that cannot be. "But, I am the foremost of sinners." You are not. The foremost of sinners died and went to heaven many years ago. His name was Saul of Tarsus, later called Paul the apostle. He was the foremost of sinners, I know he spoke the truth. "No," but you still say, "I am too wicked." You cannot be more wicked that the *foremost* of sinners. You must, at least, be second worst. Even supposing you are the worst sinner now alive, you are second worst, because Paul was foremost. But suppose you are the worst, is that not the very reason you should come to Christ?

The worse a person is, the more reason they should go to a doctor or the hospital. The poorer you are, the more reason you should accept the charity offered to you.

Christ does not want anything you have to offer. He gives freely. The worse you are, the more welcome you are. Let me ask you: Do you think you will ever get better by not coming to Christ? If you do, you know very little about the way of salvation. No, the longer you stay away, the worse you will grow. Your hope will grow weaker, your despair will become stronger. The nail with which Satan fastened you down will be more firmly clenched and you will be less hopeful than ever. Come, I implore you, remember there is nothing to be gained by delaying, but by delaying everything may be lost. "But," cries someone else, "I feel that I cannot believe." No, my friend, and you never will believe if you trust first in your believing. Remember, I am not here to invite you to faith, but to invite you to Christ. But you say, "What is the difference?" Just this: if you first say, "I want to believe something," you never do it. Your first question must be, "What is it I am to believe?" Then faith will come as the result of your searching. Our first job is not about faith, but about Christ. Come to Calvary and see the cross. Behold the Son of God, he who made the heavens and the earth, dying for your sins. Look to him, is there not power in him to save? Look at his face, so full of pity. Can you not see the love in his heart that proves him *willing* to save? The sight of Christ will help you to believe. Do not believe first and then go to Christ. That faith will be worthless. Go to Christ without any faith, and cast yourself on him, sink or swim.

I hear another cry, "Oh, you do not know how often I have been invited, nor how long I have rejected the Lord." I do not know and I do not want to know. All I know is that my Master has sent me to compel you to come in, so come now. You may have rejected a thousand invitations; do not make this the thousandth-and-one. You have heard the gospel so often that you have become gospel hardened. But do I not see a tear in your eye? Come, my friend, do not be hardened by this morning's sermon. Oh, Spirit of the living God, come and melt this heart, because it has never been melted. Compel this person to come in! I cannot let you go on such an empty excuse. If you have lived so many years slighting Christ, there are so many reasons why you should not slight him now.

Did I hear you whisper that this is not a convenient time? Then what must I say to you? When will that convenient time come? Will it come when you are in hell? Will that be a convenient time? Will it come when you are on your deathbed, and the choke of death is strangling you? Will it be your convenient time then? Or when the burning fever is scalding your brow, or when the cold clammy sweat is there, will those be convenient times? When extreme pain is torturing you, or you are on the edge of the grave? No! Now is the convenient time, this morning is the convenient time. Remember, I have no authority to ask you to come to Christ *tomorrow*. The Master has given you no invitation to come to him next Tuesday. The invitation is, "*Today*, if you hear his voice, do not harden your hearts as in the rebellion." The Holy Spirit says "today." "Come *now*, let us reason together." Why should you put it off? This may be the last warning you will ever have. Put it off now and you may never weep over your sins again; you may never have such an earnest message delivered to you. You may not be pleaded with as I am pleading with you now. You may go away, and God may say, "He is joined to idols; leave him alone." He will throw the reins on your neck and let you go your way. If that happens, mark my words, your path is certain, but it is the certain path to damnation and swift destruction.

Is my invitation all in vain? Will you not come to Christ now? What more can I do? I have one more thing I can do. I can be allowed to weep for you. I can be permitted to pray for you. You can sneer at my message if you like. You will laugh at the preacher, you will call him a fanatic if you will. He will not scold you, he will bring no accusation against you to the great Judge. As far as he is concerned the offense is forgiven before it is committed. But do remember that the message you are rejecting this morning is a message from one who loves you, it is given to you by the lips of one who loves you. You may play your soul away with the devil, to the point you think it is not important; but there lives at least one who is in earnest about your soul, one who wrestled with his God in prayer before he came here, for strength to preach to you. And when he has gone from this place, he will not forget his hearers of this morning. So, when words cannot move you, we can give tears, because words and tears are the arms with which gospel ministers compel people to come in.

You do not know, and I suppose could not believe, how concerned a man whom God has called to the ministry feels about his congregation, and especially about some of them. I heard just the other day about a young man who attended here for a long time. His father's hope was that he would be brought to Christ. However, he became acquainted with an atheist. He now neglects his business and lives in continual sin. I saw his father's poor colorless face. I did not ask him to tell me the story himself, because I felt that would stir up memories and open a sore. Sometimes I am afraid that a good man's gray hairs may be brought with sorrow to the grave. Young men, you do not pray for yourselves, but your mothers wrestle in prayer for you. You will not think about your own souls, but your father is torn up inside. I have been at prayer meetings and heard parents pray for their children. They could not have prayed with more earnestness and more intense anguish if they had been seeking their own soul's salvation. Is it not strange, that we should be ready to move heaven and earth for your salvation, and that you still have no thought for *yourselves*, no concern about eternal things?

I now turn for a moment to others who are here. There are some of you who are members of Christian churches, who make a profession of religion, but unless I am mistaken about you—and I will be happy if I am—your profession is a lie. You do not live up to it, you dishonor it. You rarely attend church services and are comfortable with that practice, not to mention sins worse than that. Now I ask you who injure the doctrine of God your Savior, do you imagine you can call me your pastor, and yet my soul does not tremble over you and weep for you in secret? It may not bother you much how you ruin the garments of your Christianity, but it is a great concern to many of God's children, who sigh and cry, and groan for the sins of the professors of Christianity.

Is there anything left for your minister to do besides weep and pray for you? Yes, there is one more thing. God has not given his servants the power to regenerate, but he has given them something close to it. It is impossible for anyone to regenerate his neighbor. Yet how are they born to God? Does not the apostle Paul write to Philemon that he became the father of Onesimus? The minister has a power given him from God, to be considered both the father and the mother of those born to God. Paul called them "my little children" and said he was "in the anguish of childbirth until Christ" was formed in them. What can we do? We can appeal to the Holy Spirit. I know I have preached the gospel and that I have preached it earnestly. I challenge my Master to honor his own promise. He has said his word "shall not return to me empty" and it will not. It is in his hands, not mine. I cannot compel you, but you oh Spirit of God, who holds the key of the heart, you can compel. Have you ever noticed, in the book of the Revelation, where it says, "Behold, I stand at the door and knock," that a few verses before, that same person is described as "the true one, who has the key of David"? So if knocking does not work, he has the key and can and will come in. If the knocking of an earnest minister does not succeed with you this morning, there still remains that secret opening of the heart by the Spirit to compel you.

It is my duty to try hard to win you, as though it was up to me. I now place the matter into my Master's hands. It cannot be his will for us to labor in childbirth and not deliver spiritual children. It is with *him.* He is master of the heart. Some of you will be compelled by sovereign grace and will become the willing captives of the all-conquering Jesus. He will use this sermon to bow your hearts before him.

Printed in Poland
by Amazon Fulfillment
Poland Sp. z o.o., Wrocław

49902070R00094